University of London
Institute of Commonwealth Studies

COMMONWEALTH PAPERS

General Editor
Professor W. H. Morris-Jones

17

The Administration of Ghana's Foreign Relations, 1957–1965:
A Personal Memoir

COMMONWEALTH PAPERS

The Administration of Ghana's Foreign Relations, 1957–1965: A Personal Memoir

by
MICHAEL DEI-ANANG
Professor of African Studies
State University of New York at Brockport

UNIVERSITY OF LONDON
Published for the
Institute of Commonwealth Studies
THE ATHLONE PRESS
1975

Published by
THE ATHLONE PRESS
UNIVERSITY OF LONDON
at 4 *Gower Street, London* W C I

Distributed by Tiptree Book Services Ltd
Tiptree, Essex

U.S.A. and Canada
Humanities Press Inc
New Jersey

© *University of London* 1975

ISBN 0 485 17617 3

Printed in Great Britain by
WESTERN PRINTING SERVICES LTD
BRISTOL

FOREWORD

Following the publication in 1972 of Sir Charles Jeffries' *Whitehall and the Colonial Service: An Administrative Memoir, 1939–1956*, the interest of the *Commonwealth Papers* series in administrative memoirs written by retired public officials is continued in Dr Michael Dei-Anang's account of the working of the Ghanaian foreign office in the Nkrumah period. Dr Dei-Anang was Principal Secretary at the Ministry of Foreign Affairs from 1959 to 1961 and Head of the African Affairs Secretariat from 1961 until the coup of 1966. Through his personal portrayal of events we are able to see several interesting features of the governmental machinery during times of change and excitement.

The Institute wishes to thank the Nuffield Foundation for their continuing interest in this kind of work and for the grant which they made to facilitate this particular publication.

W. H. M-J.

PREFACE

This brief account of the administration of the Foreign Service of Ghana under Kwame Nkrumah has been inspired by my study of works by authors who have prepared accounts on the administration of the external relations of other Commonwealth governments, particularly those of Britain, Canada, and Australia.

From the outset of that study one outstanding fact became clear to me: there was a great difference in approach and outlook between the British civil service tradition operating in Britain itself and in Canada and Australia. The basic procedures in each of the areas examined had variations due to the peculiar circumstances existing in each of the areas concerned.

It will be seen therefore, by those who are familiar with other systems, that my brief study of the administration of policy in Ghana's Foreign Service shows that there is a marked contrast between the British civil service tradition and the style of administration which Nkrumah set out to encourage. It must also be noted that, essentially, the routine processes of British colonial administration in the Gold Coast, which independent Ghana inherited, were not the same as the so-called 'Whitehall' system of administration. The Foreign Service procedures which Cumming-Bruce initiated in Ghana were much distrusted by Nkrumah as not in keeping with his African aspirations. Time and again I refer to this suspicion of the British style especially in the form in which that style is presented to the world as an organ maintained by a politically neutral body of civil servants.[1]

I have to state that I personally was sympathetic to Nkrumah's objectives in trying to break away from the British tradition. However, for me the break was not easy, because my own career embodied the two concepts of commitment. On the one hand I was anxious to maintain, and indeed did much to establish, an administration wedded to the practice of procedures by recognized routines and properly trained personnel; on the other hand I felt the need to respond to the political aspirations of my government with particular reference to its pan-African vision in so far as it evolved a clear ethos and declared objectives. The real problem I would have liked to see examined further is the extent of the practicability of maintaining a politically neutral civil service organization, because I am frankly doubtful whether such a body can exist. The British who invented that concept are hedged in by a system of conventions and a body of precedents developed over a considerable number of years. A senior civil servant in a British ministry can perform his duties knowing that his colleagues, the general public, and his political mentors recognize the operation, or at least the existence, of those conventions and precedents. It seems to me that it is the way these conventions are observed that gives the impression that the civil service cadres are politically neutral. In the case of Africa and other developing states such conventions are either absent or now being formulated and tried. While I can, therefore, appreciate the reasons for the British concept of civil service neutrality and would not condemn it outright as Nkrumah perhaps uncritically did by regarding it as a tool for serving 'the interests of a foreign power', I would exercise caution in adopting it wholesale in an African milieu.

If the African civil servant identifies the situation in this manner, he will not hesitate to maintain a commitment and dedication to those policies of his government that are in the interests of the general public while using his western-style training and experience to resist those which appear to him not in the public interest. It would be optimistic to suppose that such resistance could always produce positive results, as the incident referred to in the last chapter of this study exemplifies. Until the conventions and precedents mentioned above have secure roots in Africa, the civil servant must be content to believe that his conscience is the best judge in the situation in which an 'African flavour' in administration sometimes constitutes the abandonment of restraint and correct procedures. For the time being then the real challenge which the African official has to face is related to the need to define clearly the content of that 'African flavour' in administration. Perhaps it will require more than a generation to achieve this, if the experience of other countries is anything to go by.

It will be seen from my text that there was a change of tone and tempo after 1962 and that when the domestic situation began to show signs of strain resulting from the faulty performance of the government in the agricultural and industrial sectors the thrill and excitement of combining my dual commitment to preservation and innovation in administration gave way to anxiety and frustration.

At the time of the coup in 1966 the problem of evolving a Foreign Service administration with a purely African flavour in consonance with national objectives and aspirations had yet to be resolved. Failure to do this was due to several factors, such as the uneasy relationships between politicians and civil servants, weaknesses in the party system of the CPP, and the peculiar temperament of Nkrumah. The present officials have therefore the great task and responsibility of ensuring that they begin the search for an African system of administration which embodies all the essential characteristics of efficient processes of management and the features of African temperament that may be considered particularly unique and deserving of emphasis and development.

This study was prepared principally from my personal recollections of various events which had a bearing on my day-to-day work as an administrator. It is unfortunate that my official diaries, which contained a very careful documentation of daily events and the reasons and motivations for decisions, covering more than five years' service in Flagstaff House under the late Dr Kwame Nkrumah, were lost in the 1966 military *coup d'état*, when I was with the President in Peking.

I am therefore especially grateful to those of my former colleagues, including Mr A. L. Adu and Mr K. B. Asante, and other experts on African affairs, such as Mr Thomas Hodgkin and Dr Henry L. Bretton, who read this work in manuscript and made very candid and much valued suggestions for improvement.

To Mr J. M. Lee and Professor W. H. Morris-Jones of the Institute of Commonwealth Studies, University of London, I must express my most sincere thanks for much advice and assistance in the execution of this very challenging assignment.

M.D-A.

CONTENTS

A CIVIL SERVANT UNDER NKRUMAH

This study describes my experience as a public servant in administering the external relations of Ghana, which was the first British territory south of the Sahara to gain its independence.

In the chapters that follow, two processes of administration are presented. The first is that represented by the operation of a diplomatic organization based on training and techniques acquired by sending selected Ghanaian officers to Britain on attachment to the Commonwealth Relations Office and the Foreign Office to attend courses at the London School of Economics. The second process is the simultaneous employment of two or more parallel agencies under the direct personal supervision of the head of state. Scott Thompson has argued that by the summer of 1962 the mechanism of parallel agencies duplicating each other, although correct in organizational terms, had in fact been replaced by 'only one network with power—with the Bureau of African Affairs at its apex'.[2] My own account analyses the parts played by the other agencies in the field, the Ministry of Foreign Affairs and the African Affairs Secretariat. My career from 1959 to 1966 lay in these two organizations, and my aim is to give some indication of the problems faced by career civil servants.

In 1957, the year of independence, the new Ministry of Foreign Affairs was set up. Unlike Canada, Australia, or India, Ghana did not describe its Foreign Office as a Ministry of External Affairs. It is significant also that from independence the Prime Minister himself took over the foreign relations portfolio. As Minister in charge of Foreign Affairs, Nkrumah organized the first conference of independent African States. His grant of a loan of £10 million to save Guinea from collapse, and to bring it into a union with Ghana, was arranged when he was Minister in charge. From the beginning his personality dominated Ghana's external relations, because he felt that he had a specific mission for Africa which could be fully realized only under his control at the helm.

When I was appointed Permanent Secretary of the Ministry of Foreign Affairs in the last quarter of 1959, Ako Adjei had become Foreign Minister. At this time Nkrumah's role in the department's affairs was less obvious but no less strong. The Minister and I very often attended prolonged meetings with the Prime Minister to discuss subjects of concern to the Ministry and to submit memoranda for his consideration on matters which one would have thought normally within the purview of the Foreign Minister; in order to ensure that his African objectives were properly developed, it seems clear that he needed personal involvement in the more important aspects of work in the Foreign Ministry.

NKRUMAH'S INFLUENCE

What was Nkrumah's form of administration and how did it affect the role of the bureaucrats in the Foreign Office? Being summoned to work frequently in Flagstaff House, as I was, I soon observed that Nkrumah was very critical of the Ministry's handling of problems; now and again he dropped broad hints that the Office did not have an adequate sense of urgency; that it could not anticipate events; that he was getting tired of having to make constant enquiries about what the Ministry had done or proposed to do.

Nkrumah's impatience reflected his desire for active involvement in Africa's destiny, because 1959 was a year of great activity, and it seemed that the whole business of government—in so far as Ghana's external relations were concerned—centred round his movements. In that year he paid official visits to India, the UAR, Nigeria, the Cameroons, Guinea, Liberia, and the United Kingdom. Each visit required a great deal of planning and organization. Because he expected the best, always believing that what happened in Ghana was an inspiration to other Africans emerging from colonial rule, it was difficult to get him to count the cost, in terms of either the human material available, or the limited resources at the disposal of a small country such as Ghana. His reaction to considerations of cost and expense was that Ghana should be given the best—damn the cost—for in all history no government had been 'imprisoned for its national debt'.

There is no sign of orthodoxy here; no responsible person, nor nation state, can embark on any programme of development without counting the cost; when one is dealing with the fate and fortunes of a whole nation the importance of making a clear and detailed analysis of the human and material resources involved cannot be over-emphasized. This contempt for routine and red-tape was sometimes allowed to touch such extremes of illogicality. In his dealings with the 'hardy annuals' of corruption, imperialism, colonialism, and neo-colonialism, it seems that he often used the 'multiple audience' technique: when he condemned corruption in his public speeches in Parliament and elsewhere he meant it for internal consumption; on the other hand, his condemnation of colonialism 'and its cohorts' was usually intended for consumption abroad. The enigma of his life was the ability to carry everyone with him, wherever he was. At all times he was determined to succeed, whatever the circumstances. By temperament and disposition he was opposed to the view that it is far better to fail conventionally than to succeed unconventionally.

Another example of this attitude of mind may be observed from his decision to have put up within ten months a complex of new buildings comprising a set of self-contained suites for over thirty heads of state, a conference auditorium, and a banqueting hall for the Organization of African Unity Conference in 1965. Nkrumah came to this decision after the 1964 OAU Conference in Cairo had agreed to hold the 1965 meeting in Accra.[3] By all the rules of construction it was difficult to conceive how these buildings could have been completed in time for the Conference: apart from swish, water, timber, and labour, practically every component had to be imported. He was, however, undeterred by this and lost no time in discussing his ideas with Adegbite, the Ghanaian architect. Adegbite was then instructed to produce working plans within the shortest possible time. My colleagues and I in the Secretariat, and at least one senior Cabinet Minister, had expressed doubts about the practicability, if not the wisdom, of this proposal but Nkrumah maintained his optimism.

In spite of this, Amonoo, Asante, and myself set to work and secretly prepared an alternative plan for housing the delegates and using Parliament House as the conference hall. Meanwhile, construction proceeded according to the Nkrumah plan. Now and again members of the diplomatic corps from the independent African states who had heard of the decisions pestered our office with enquiries about the progress of the building. Each time we assured them of satisfactory progress. They were sceptical. No-one should have worried. A couple of weeks before the date of the Conference, 'Job 600', as the OAU complex came to be known, was completed at a reputed cost of some eight million pounds and in the week before the Conference the Secretariat was instructed to arrange a pre-Conference dinner in the banqueting hall.

What was to happen to these buildings after the Conference? Nkrumah's idea was that they would be offered to the OAU as accommodation for its Secretariat. However, before the offer could be made, and a few days before the Conference was due to meet in Accra, news came that the Emperor of Ethiopia had provided permanent buildings in Addis Ababa for the same purpose. In any case, there is sufficient evidence for the view that in Nkrumah's thinking the complex of buildings could provide accommodation for the headquarters of the 'Union Government of Africa', if Ghana could maintain the initiative on this.

When Nkrumah made a brief stop in Cairo on his mission to Hanoi, the late President Nasser asked in a private conversation to what use he proposed to put those fine buildings in Accra. It was not a rhetorical question, but I cannot recall the answer. Thus 'Job 600' may add to the architectural beauty of Accra but in the absence of Nkrumah it has been converted to 'serve as offices for a number of government ministries / departments and international organizations like the Association of African Universities'.[4]

His capacity for work was enormous, as was his desire for innovation, but the combination of these factors, buttressed by his impatience to have all his tomorrows today, made work under Nkrumah seem like running a non-stop factory. It was not unusual for him to telephone me at dead of night suggesting that a new idea that had just occurred to him might be made the subject of a memorandum for discussion at a meeting next day.

PARALLEL AGENCIES

The second process of administration to be described in these chapters, the employment of parallel agencies, was the product of Nkrumah's decision to work through the Bureau of African Affairs created in 1959 and the African Affairs Secretariat established in 1961,[5] as well as through the Ministry itself. The relationship between these three bodies was the major feature in the administration of foreign policy after 1961.

The African Affairs Secretariat and the Foreign Ministry undertook purely diplomatic duties in Ghana's relations with external powers in Africa and outside the continent, respectively. The Secretariat dealt mainly with African problems. To Nkrumah Africa was the basic area of external policy, all activities outside Africa being designed principally to promote the objectives of the African cause.

For the liberation struggle in Africa, the Bureau of African Affairs was Nkrumah's sole instrument. Freedom fighters from every part of Africa found their way there. Many of the well-known characters in the anti-colonial struggle, such as Joshua Nkomo, Ndabaningi Sithole, and Amilcar Cabral, came to Ghana. These as well as the nationalists of Angola, Mozambique, and South West Africa needed financial assistance, medical supplies, and advice on guerilla strategy to fight the colonialists. Nkomo and Sithole were running rival parties—ZAPU and ZANU respectively—on which each relied to bring about the overthrow of white minority rule in Rhodesia. Nkrumah's exhortation to close their ranks in the common struggle proved of no avail. Their failure to collaborate caused a serious breach in efforts to liberate their country. Eventually, as is now well known, they both ended in detention in Rhodesia where they have remained for many years. The Bureau maintained a number of training camps to help nationalists and their followers. In 1966, after Nkrumah's overthrow in the military coup, all sorts of statements were made about the use to which Foreign Service officers, myself and others, put these camps. In actual fact, only certain Foreign Service officers knew of the existence of the training camps, and often this knowledge was acquired indirectly. This point is supported by K. B. Asante who was for most of the period between 1961 and 1966 Principal Secretary of the African Affairs Secretariat.

Nkrumah would often stand before a large map of Africa and, surveying its size, say something like this: Africa has such land mass that our continent alone could take comfortably the whole of the United States of America, Britain, Ireland, Europe, Japan and its islands, India, New Zealand, and still leave room for more. Consider Africa's mineral and agricultural products—oil, iron ore, diamonds, copper, tin, uranium, gold, cocoa, tobacco, rubber, and others too numerous to mention. What do we lack? And why should we be so poor in the midst of such plenty?

Nkrumah's commitment to Africa was total; the time and circumstances in Africa favoured the cause he tried to promote. The political climate of the post-war world and the liberal tendencies to which it gave rise helped to arouse sympathy for the process of decolonization. Imperialism was becoming an embarrassment, and the concept of the Commonwealth had succeeded that of Empire. By identifying himself closely with these liberal forces and seeking to secure allies for the cause wherever they could be found, Nkrumah succeeded in making little Ghana the focus of world attention. A new dimension was given to the very concept of Africanness itself.

In the course of developing his African programme Nkrumah maintained a remarkably wide circle of international relationships. These included world statesmen, philosophers, political and economic scientists, captains of industry, and other public figures. His exchange of views with thinkers and industrialists such as the late Bertrand Russell, Edgar Kaiser, Barbara Ward, and General Edward Spears was constant, sustained, and constructive. Such consultations could have given the impression of Nkrumah's lack of originality as Ali Mazrui has implied in his 'Nkrumah—the Leninist Czar'.[6] In actual fact he sought to ascertain the views of those he held in high esteem in order to assist the formulation of his own views on questions of national importance. These contacts should therefore be seen as a necessary part of the process of policy-making.

Nkrumah became an implacable opponent of regionalism in Africa. He regarded it as another form of 'balkanization' and always contrasted it sharply with the advantages likely to accrue to Africa from a pan-African relationship. Robert Gardiner, the Ghanaian Executive Secretary of the United Nations Economic Committee for Africa, was not the only one to be confronted in this way with Nkrumah's strong anti-regionalist views. The main source of strain between Nyerere and Nkrumah stemmed from their opposing views on regionalism. Oginga Odinga records his encounter with Nkrumah on this issue as follows:

> At Accra Airport I sensed afresh the spirit of nationalism and African Brotherhood abroad in the new Party ... when we met again, Nkrumah and I embraced. His visions of a Union of African States were as vivid as ever. We argued hotly, though, on the organization of African regional groupings. I advocated a regional grouping for East Africa on the grounds that we shared a common history and colonial overlordship, common language, problems and goals. Nkrumah was apprehensive that a federation with internal difficulties would engross our attention, and cause us to neglect the goal of broader African unity.[7]

The extent to which the *coup* in Uganda has strained inter-regional relations in East Africa and almost created a serious impasse at the OAU seems to bear out some of Nkrumah's fears about regional groupings. Differences in approach between the UN Economic Commission for Africa and Nkrumah might have arisen from the fact that the UN regarded the whole of Africa as a region, accepting the major sections of Africa, such as East and West, as sub-regions. In this sense, any kind of regional approach to African problems would have been a violation of Nkrumah's view of continental unity. Indeed, in his view, the ECA, being both financially and administratively under UN control, was not strictly an African organ. When Robert Gardiner called on Nkrumah at Flagstaff House during a brief visit to Ghana, I was summoned to his office to be informed that 'Kweku had been baptised again for the cause'. But Gardiner took his leave with deliberate steps from Nkrumah's office, and as he gained a respectable distance away from the Osagyefo, said to me *sotto voce* 'a baptism of fire'.

CIVIL SERVICE PRINCIPLES

Nkrumah pressed for action to invigorate the administrative and diplomatic machine for its growing responsibilities. Periodic conferences of heads of missions were held in Accra to acquaint them with developments in policy at home but it appears that headquarters staff needed greater opportunity to learn about problems confronting their colleagues in the field. As the Foreign Office had no inspectorate staff and officials at base were too occupied with their own problems of administration to analyse and evaluate field reports, such conferences were invaluable for securing improvements in work.

Nkrumah's confidence in the ability of his government to carry out successfully the liberation struggle in Africa was near-absolute. He therefore expected the civil service machine to identify itself completely with his government's aspirations.

The main problem, however, was that the Ghanaian civil service was a product of the colonial administration which had taught the importance of observing a code of conduct in administration based on approved regulations. Nearly every activity of government had to be weighed and considered against them. To continue this tradition is not sabotage, or a slavish imitation of any foreign traditions. It is no desire to uphold what has been termed as the Whitehall tradition of 'career neutrality'. As W. G. Fleming has pointed out, 'the Civil Service of Great Britain from Walpole to Peel, and that of the United States after the advent of Jacksonian democracy were highly politicised'.[8] The colonial tradition of administration however required adaptation and Ghana's experience after 1961 shows the agony of this process. Within the ruling party, the Convention People's Party, the rise to power of a group associated with NASSO (the National Association of Socialist Student Organizations) brought established administrators into conflict on two fronts. First, the new group succeeded in removing or discrediting prominent politicians, such as Gbedemah, Botsio, Krobo Edusei, and others who in the early days of the CPP had contributed much to the stability and power of the party either through their political organization or by loyalty to Nkrumah but were now regarded as obstacles to socialist reconstruction. The group began also to challenge the system of career appointments to the higher ranks of the civil service by emphasizing the need for ideological competence as a necessary factor in the maintenance of the government's policies. Second, the new group's influence in foreign policy was against more orthodox diplomatic practice which seemed to them to be an unnecessary drag on vigorous action. My purpose is to indicate how civil service principles are regarded when they are opposed by such obvious challenges.

As Principal Secretary of the Ministry from 1959 to 1961 I was directly concerned with the maintenance of the rules governing the career service. The post brought me important responsibilities in administrative control and over establishment questions in the Foreign

Service. As Head of the African Affairs Secretariat from 1961 to 1966 I was also in daily contact with the problems faced by career diplomats, although I was obviously required to devote most of my time to questions of strategy and tactics in tendering advice to the President or in executing his instructions. My change of role in 1961 therefore corresponds to the general change of climate in Ghanaian politics. The situation was full of contradictions. All I can do in this study is to show some of the points of tension.

Thomas Hodgkin has indicated the variety of contradictions— 'between factions within the party; between interests on which the party depended for support; between the party and para-party organizations; between the party and the great estates of the realm, the Civil Service, the Army, the judiciary, the academics, etc.; between orthodox diplomacy and revolutionary diplomacy; between external influences (political, military, religious, cultural, commercial) and their representatives within the Ghana system . . . no doubt the CPP was a petty bourgeois party. No doubt it failed to carry through a socialist revolution, but it affected the course of African history in significant ways, which remain to be understood'.[9]

I wish to show how administrative support for the aspirations and policies of African governments must not deny the framework of established norms and principles. The new African states must endeavour to establish administrative conventions that can be accepted, whatever government is in power. This would help to produce a stable and consistent cadre of civil servants, who would know that whatever they support and respect in the course of their administrative responsibilities is done in the interest of the nation as a whole not as a particular fad or a personal wish based on narrow considerations which offend against the public interest. I hope the following chapters will show both my desire to accept certain principles of administration within the colonial tradition, and also my intense longing for the exercise of the innovative powers of the African bureaucrat. This apparent existence between two worlds is the very core of the problem of administration in Africa today. It appears quite clearly in my own experience, as one brought up in a colonial order through which I learnt to accept certain codes of administrative conduct. On the other hand, as I passed into the new order of African independence, I became aware of the need to search in the past for any strands of a peculiarly African identity with which to enrich the sum total of our national heritage. Although my study does not cover the identification of an African style of administration, I cannot see that this sort of ambivalence should be deprecated. It is only when the application of the foreign norms militates against development that there can be any rational sense in questioning them.[10]

In a sense the new African states, whether they be French or English-speaking, have themselves this tradition of a double world, a dual existence, from which they can draw the best only if they are ready to show a keen sense of discrimination in making their choices.

PROBLEMS OF POLICY-MAKING AND THE MACHINERY OF ORTHODOX DIPLOMACY

Among the new ministries established under the 1951 constitutional changes was one for Defence and External Affairs (MDEA) whose Head of Department was the 'Chief Secretary' of the colonial administration. He and all his subordinate officers, except the auxiliary executive and clerical grades, were overseas officers. In 1951, while working in the Department of Education as a Senior Education Officer, I was posted to this new Ministry for training with the rank of Senior Assistant Secretary (Supernumerary), the term 'supernumerary' implying that I was understudying an overseas officer with a view to taking over from him on proving my capacity for the new responsibilities. For the first six months I was the only African officer in that grade, and my responsibility was the Imperial War Graves Commission. In spite of its nomenclature, the Ministry had no real international responsibilities of a political nature. It could not be said that I was receiving formal diplomatic training nor was the service more than a hypothetical foreign service organization. This is the reason why it became necessary to make special facilities available for training staff for the future Ghanaian Ministry of Foreign Affairs.

PREPARING FOR INDEPENDENCE

Before independence, in order to expand the process of Africanization, I was transferred to work with A. L. Adu in a new Training and Recruitment Office responsible for preparing and recruiting Africans for appointment to senior posts in the Home Service. In 1953, four years before independence, the government appointed a four-man committee to review the Africanization of the public service. That committee made the following self-explanatory comment in one of its reports to the government:

Under the existing promotion policy it is difficult for Africans to rise early to these levels [i.e. the directing and policy-making positions] by promotion in the ordinary course, since, for the time being, the senior and experienced officers in the old senior service are mostly overseas officers.[11]

Even at this stage the Ghanaian civil service was not sufficiently reorganized in domestic departments to fit it for its new role and responsibilities as a predominantly African service. One can therefore understand why special measures were necessary for the establishment of a Foreign Service.

With the agreement of the government of Ghana, the Commonwealth Relations Office appointed an expert to undertake the training of a team of Ghanaian candidates for eventual appointment to the Foreign Service. The official appointed was Francis Cumming-Bruce. By September 1955 some eighteen new men had been selected through the Public Service Commission from the numerous applications received. The first candidates were recruited in the following groups:

1. H. A. H. Grant
2. R. A. Quarshie
3. Major S. K. Anthony

4. A. B. B. Kofi
5. Alex Quaison-Sackey
6. F. S. Arkhurst
7. K. S. Dadzie
8. R. M. Akwei
9. F. E. Boaten
10. H. R. Amonoo
11. E. M. Debrah
12. S. P. O. Kumi
13. K. B. Asante
14. H. V. Sekyi
15. O. H. Brew

16. Kwame Addae
17. S. E. Quarm
18. G. H. Arthur

The more senior officers in these groups were sent on attachment to British embassies and high commissions after brief orientation courses at the Foreign Office and the Commonwealth Relations Office in London. The others were sent to the London School of Economics for a six months course before their allocation to British missions overseas and by 1956 they were posted to British diplomatic missions overseas. Their training included a study of diplomatic relations, problems of diplomatic immunity, telex and code systems of communication, protocol matters, and external publicity. At the head of the new service the government appointed A. L. Adu, an experienced Ghanaian official who was among the first African officers to be promoted to the

rank of District Commissioner in the political administration of the
Gold Coast. His own orientation included a year's course at the
Imperial Defence College. The record of achievement of these officers
proves beyond doubt that their selection was justified. The following
are the present occupations of thirteen of them:

H. R. Amonoo	formerly Ambassador to the United States; now accredited to Bonn
R. M. Akwei	Ambassador to the People's Republic of China
S. K. Anthony	Retired; formerly High Commissioner in Canada
F. S. Arkhurst	Academic work in the United States after retirement as Ghana's representative at the United Nations
K. B. Asante	Deputy Secretary, National Redemption Council, Accra
O. H. Brew	Retired; formerly Ambassador to Senegal
F. E. Boaten	Ghana's Representative at the United Nations
K. K. S. Dadzie	United Nations Secretariat
E. M. Debrah	Secretary, National Redemption Council, Accra
S. E. Quarm	Ambassador to the United States
R. A. Quarshie	Minister of Trade in Busia regime until its overthrow
A. Quaison-Sackey	Barrister, Accra. Previously President of the United Nations General Assembly, 1964, and Foreign Minister, 1965
H. V. Sekyi	High Commissioner in United Kingdom

From independence Nkrumah entertained misgivings about the
Foreign Service.[12] He had doubts about its capacity to interpret his
African policies with his own vigour and vision. It was unrealistic to
expect British training of the new Ghana Foreign Service personnel to
be marked by any degree of enthusiasm for decolonization: Nkrumah
was neither foolish nor naive enough to believe that Britain would
train Africans in anti-imperialist tactics. With his declaration of the
policy of total liberation from colonial rule, Nkrumah could not overlook the fact that Britain was one of the two countries with the largest
colonial territories in Africa. If he had had his way, he might have
wished that his first team of Foreign Service officers had been trained
elsewhere than in Britain. On the other hand, their training in Britain
had some advantages. Britain was a great world power and her capital
was a busy nerve centre and a useful listening post in international
affairs.

Nkrumah in 1957 invited George Padmore to take up a post as
adviser to the Prime Minister on African Affairs.[13] Adu, as the new

Permanent Secretary for Foreign Affairs, argued strongly against such an appointment on the ground that Padmore was not competent to advise Nkrumah on African affairs because he had not lived in Africa.[14] Nkrumah was more concerned with Padmore's pan-African experience, which was at that time a new field for Adu. Thus from the very beginning there was a strong difference of outlook between Nkrumah and his Foreign Service.*

* Adu's comment on this portion of my account, reflecting his initial disagreement with George Padmore and with Thompson's interpretation of the situation, is worth quoting in full. It emphasizes the dichotomy that existed between Adu and Nkrumah on the significance of Padmore in Nkrumah's political strategy in Africa. Perhaps it can be said that at the time of Adu's opposition he had inadequate information about Padmore's background. Obviously, the fact that Padmore 'had never lived in Africa' was irrelevant. He was already well-known as an anti-colonial fighter:

'I argued strongly against Padmore's appointment, on the ground that I did not consider that Padmore was competent to advise Nkrumah on African affairs, since as far as I knew, he had never lived in Africa nor had he been involved in any of the African nationalist movements within Africa. It took some time before Nkrumah defined the role Padmore was to play, namely, to head an office outside the orthodox government machinery to carry through his policy for the emancipation of those parts of Africa still under foreign rule and therefore to work with nationalist movements and political parties, an area of activity which it would be inappropriate for civil servants to engage in at that time.

'Once he made his position clear, I not only withdrew my opposition but in fact collaborated enthusiastically in getting his office established, including negotiating for a vote for him. However, Padmore did not forget that I had opposed his appointment initially and this dogged our personal relationships for some time. It was not until after the first Conference of Independent African States that, over a minor crisis, the two of us were finally reconciled at a meeting with Nkrumah. Thereafter, our relations, and also the relations between the Ministry of Foreign Affairs during my tenure and the Bureau of African Affairs became one of healthy collaboration on the basis of clearly defined roles.

'One more comment on this chapter: I believe it is a little of an exaggeration to say that there was a strong difference of outlook between Nkrumah and his Foreign Service. I can say that the Service was constantly seeking to know what Nkrumah expected of it and to organize itself to respond.

'The prejudice against the so-called colonial mentality of civil servants generally was, however, very strong. The difference was therefore more imaginary on the part of the politicians than real. I recall Nkrumah's deep uneasiness about the Foreign Service's competence to organize the first Conference of Independent African States because of his belief that the Service, including me, was not tuned in to the African movement. He even tried to recruit an Indian diplomat, Dr Appadorai 'Secretary-General of the Indian Council of Foreign Affairs' to take charge of the arrangements. However, he was very generous in his tribute to the Foreign Service when the Conference proved that it had measured up to all that was required of it and that, in comparison with the officials from the other seven African states who later joined the Conference Secretariat, our officials stood out in terms of their ability and grasp of the objectives that the Conference sought to achieve.'

This is the background against which Nkrumah conceived the idea of maintaining two parallel organizations within the Foreign Service: one on orthodox diplomatic lines, while the other was to be given new life in the old setting of his pan-African experience. There was accordingly a new scope for collaboration with Padmore by which they hoped to continue their work for Africa in an African setting. Unfortunately for Nkrumah the link with Padmore was short-lived, for Padmore died suddenly in 1959 during a brief visit to Britain. The idea of developing two parallel services was, however, retained.

Whereas Nkrumah was not particularly enthusiastic about the training given by Britain, he showed marked interest and confidence in the Foreign Service system of India. It was one of the first countries he visited after Ghana's independence. At this time he sought and obtained from the Indian government the services of an Intelligence Officer who gave considerable assistance in the setting up of an Intelligence service unit in Ghana. In the early stages of independence, Ghanaian representatives at international conferences were advised to support the Indian line on anti-colonialism, especially at the United Nations. Furthermore, in 1959 Nkrumah had arrangements made for me to be attached to the Indian government in order to study something of the administration of its Ministry of External Affairs, together with procedures for the running of the household in the Presidential Palace in New Delhi. As a result of that visit certain administrative changes were adopted in the Ghanaian Foreign Ministry.

The Indian experience was very stimulating to me. In the Presidential household I was struck to discover that the Secretary was a military officer, Major-General Bahadur Singh. The Security Officers who were introduced to me were all military personnel. I very quickly made myself familiar with the routine running of the Palace, including procedures for receiving guests and presentation of letters of credence by diplomats, some basic details of which I was able to incorporate into the system adopted in Ghana. Attachment to the household afforded me an invaluable opportunity to meet some very distinguished Indian and other personalities, for within the household there was a little theatre with an attractive stage and facilities for showing films and presenting various kinds of Indian traditional dancing. It was here that I was introduced to Mrs Pandit, sister of Prime Minister Nehru and former President of the United Nations General Assembly. During my work at the Palace, I had perhaps one of the rarest opportunities ever to come the way of a visitor like myself in being able to meet in person the Dalai Lama who had escaped from Tibet to seek refuge in India when his territory was overrun by China.

My impressions of the External Affairs Ministry were no less vivid.

The Ministry at this time had two top-ranking Secretaries, one of them, Mr Desai, being responsible entirely for Commonwealth affairs. An officer of Principal Secretary rank dealt with information matters and held periodical press conferences to explain external problems of the Ministry, as a matter of policy, to the general public. I thought that this was an extremely useful practice in a country the size of India and with delicate problems—lingusitic, political, economic—and boundary issues affecting her sensitive neighbours.

I did not, however, miss the sight of loads of dusty files in the Ministry. Were all these the relics of the colonial past? If so, why had they survived twelve years of an independent nationalist government? The Secretary-General was busy preparing Cabinet memoranda on the Indo-Chinese border dispute and the general atmosphere was choked and charged with the danger of a military outbreak between the two great Asian states. For Nehru in particular, with India's declared policy of non-violence, this was a grave and impending doom.

Some of the changes made in Ghana after my 1959 visit to India may be summarized as follows:

(a) Establishment of a direct telephone link between the Foreign Ministry, the Prime Minister's Office, and the Governor-General's Office in the State House, to facilitate coordination of protocol duties;

(b) Maintenance of a 24-hour service for dealing with incoming and outgoing telegrams;

(c) Intensification of training of special secretaries for overseas missions leading to discharge of non-Ghanaian secretaries employed in Ghanaian missions in sensitive areas of work;

(d) Emphasis on the sensible application of the Ministry's resources in manpower and material; coupled with this a more careful scrutiny was exercised over the activities of the various divisions of the Ministry in order to secure close compliance with approved policy.

The period between 1957 and 1960 saw the functioning of a dual authority, that of the Governor-General, representing the Queen, as head of state, and that of the Prime Minister, as head of government. The position of the Queen as Ghana's head of state during this period had notable repercussions. Ambassadors-designate nominated by their governments for service in Ghana were technically accredited to the Court of St James and could not, as such, be appointed without the Queen's approval. In my experience, proposals submitted to the Queen for such appointments were never reversed but the procedure sometimes caused embarrassment in Accra, especially in the case of diplomatic appointments from the Francophone African states. The latter could not reconcile Ghana's strong anti-colonial stand with what seemed to be capitulation to British control. Administratively the procedure involved very little delay but politically it proved rather a difficult pill to swallow and it was certainly among the factors that impelled the government to work for the establishment of a republic.

DIPLOMATIC SERVICE STRUCTURE

The main structure of the diplomatic service was not changed after the republican constitution had removed the embarrassment of consulting 'the Palace' in London. But its recruitment and training were of course strictly separate from the arrangements made in the Bureau of African Affairs.

First, there was *Branch A*, entry to which was through the Public Service Commission procedure; the basic qualification for selection to this grade was a recognized university degree. Originally only male candidates were recruited into Branch A; at the time of preparing this study there were at least three women in this grade (one of them a barrister, another an economist).

Secondly, there was *Branch B*. For this grade candidates were selected by interview. Promotions to certain grades within the Branch were, however, by examination.

Thirdly, there was the *Secretarial Class*. Selection to this class was also by means of Public Service Commission procedure through prescribed aptitude and proficiency tests in shorthand, typing, and secretarial practice. The secretarial class belonged to a separate service and recruitment for it was made for the Home and Foreign Services. For this grade the government provided secretarial training in schools in Accra, Sekondi-Takoradi, Tarkwa, Kumasi, and Tamale. Exceptional secretaries were selected for training overseas to enable them either to acquire a second language or to fit them for higher responsibility in key secretarial positions as secretaries to high commissioners and ambassadors. This system produced quite satisfactory results. Below the secretarial grade there was a large pool of clerical and semi-skilled grades. There was also the special grade of security officers. Clerical officers were at first recruited locally but as every mission tended to be plagued by security problems Ghanaian nationals were increasingly used on a temporary form of recruitment without pension or allowances. This tended to engender dissatisfaction and frustration.

There was no formal institutional training for Branch A officers; this was considered essential later and, from 1961 onwards, the nucleus of an Institute of Public Administration was set up in Achimota to train senior cadres for the entire civil service. Recently, training at the Institute has been expanded to include lectures in international affairs and diplomacy, subjects that are of direct interest to the Foreign Service. The United Nations greatly assisted its growth financially and by the secondment of an experienced Indian public servant, S. Bapat, as the Institution's first Principal.

Before ambassadors took up posts abroad, they were given *ad hoc* briefing by experienced departmental officers, by Ministers, and sometimes by the President himself on the areas they were assigned to, on protocol, on procedures within the Ministry, etc.

DEPARTMENTAL ORGANIZATION

The Ministry of Foreign Affairs had overall responsibility for the general direction and control of the Ministry. From 1957 to 1965 the following Cabinet members served as Foreign Ministers: Nkrumah himself, Ako Adjei (April 1959–August 1962), Kojo Botsio (November 1958–April 1959 and March 1963–June 1965), and Alex Quaison-Sackey (June 1965–February 1966). Under the 1957 Constitution the Minister was appointed by the Governor-General on the advice of the Prime Minister, and was given overall authority, subject to the overriding powers of the Premier and the ultimate control of Parliament, for the running of his Ministry.[15]

Routine administration was the responsibility of the official head. Disciplinary problems likely to result in the dismissal of any officer were referred to the Public Service Commission through the Principal Secretary. This clear-cut definition of the lines of control and discipline was intended to insulate the service from the vagaries of political patronage.

In carrying out the responsibilities of his office the Foreign Minister was directly responsible to the Prime Minister/President. Assisting the Foreign Minister in his duties was a political colleague who held the rank of Minister of State or Deputy Minister of Foreign Affairs (see chart overleaf).

The Permanent or Principal Secretary of the Foreign Ministry was head of the Foreign Service with the rank of ambassador. The following officers held the post between 1957 and 1965: A. L. Adu, M. F. Dei-Anang, A. B. B. Kofi, and Fred Arkhurst. By virtue of his position, the Principal Secretary was required to give instructions to field officers. This was sometimes resented by ambassadors and high commissioners, especially those among them who were political appointees and not career diplomats. This is understandable, where these ambassadors were drawn from the ranks of the party in power and of the same political vintage as Ministers. But the discipline of the service was such that all classes of diplomats had to observe the same code of Foreign

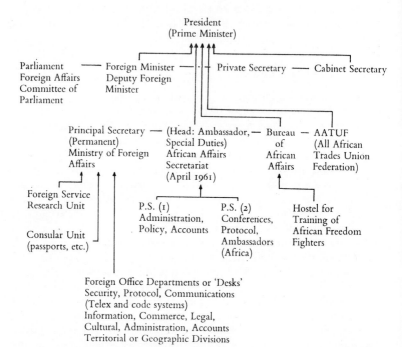

MINISTRY OF FOREIGN AFFAIRS

Organizational Chart (1957–1965)

Note: On this table K. B. Asante, who was the first of two Principal Secretaries in the African Affairs Secretariat, has commented as follows: 'For most of the period there was only one Principal Secretary and an Ambassador, Special Duties, who was Head of the Secretariat. It might also be useful to indicate that originally the Foriegn Ministry handled administration including accounts, etc. and protocol matters for the African Affairs Secretariat. The Secretariat was at that time mainly concerned with policy. Later, however, it was found from practical experience that administration could not be completely separated from policy, and moreover the Foreign Ministry could not be relied upon to keep up with the pace of work and outlook demanded by Nkrumah.' In regard to this last point I have pointed out elsewhere in extenuation that the location of the Ministry some distance away from Flagstaff House was not conducive to any reasonable attempts to 'keep up' with Nkrumah's pace and outlook.

Service regulations. By 1961 there were virtually two independent official heads in charge of Foreign Affairs at the Foreign Ministry and at the African Affairs Secretariat, as the chart shows.

There was no case of transfer from the field of politics to that of the career stream below ambassadorial level, owing to the rigid qualifications required for entry to the career structure. On the other hand there is at least one example of the transfer of a career diplomat to a political post. Alex Quaison-Sackey was elected Member of Parliament and subsequently appointed a Cabinet Minister.

Under the Principal Secretary was a team of official colleagues consisting of Branch A and Branch B officers together with supporting secretarial and clerical staffs. As indicated in the chart, the head of each division or 'desk' worked to the Principal Secretary. In urgent cases, as determined by the Minister, or in his absence by the Principal Secretary, the head of branch could submit his work direct to the Foreign Minister. The functional divisions in addition to providing services for the Ministry personnel also performed political, consular, and other duties for the state as a whole.

It was a principle of discipline and control in the Ministry that no branch or 'desk' head should sign any outgoing letters. All such letters, whether personally dealt with by the Principal Secretary or not, were signed for him over his official title. In certain cases, such as letters rejecting requests from heads of diplomatic missions, our own or foreign ambassadors, it was a standing rule that the Principal Secretary, or in extreme cases the Minister himself, should personally sign the letter. It is fair to indicate that this clearly defined chain of responsibility originated from procedures established before independence!

BANDUNG AND THE PROGRAMME OF DECOLONIZATION

While the orthodox lines of diplomacy based on the organization of the Foreign Ministry described above were in the process of development, a parallel system under the Bureau of African Affairs, aiming at establishing a programme for decolonization, was simultaneously at work. My personal experience soon made it clear to me that, as far as Nkrumah was concerned, the decolonization process was more important than diplomatic relationships.

The Afro-Asian Conference in Bandung brought Nkrumah his first real opportunity to exercise overt diplomacy in the area of decolonization. In 1955 the Prime Minister of Indonesia, Dr Sastroamijojo, invited the Gold Coast to attend the Bandung Conference of Afro-Asian States. The Colonial Office agreed on condition that the Gold Coast representatives attended as observers. Kojo Botsio led the delegation. As Secretary to the delegation I was responsible for preparing[16] the travel plan. We travelled through Lome, Paris, Rome, and Bombay to Singapore. We were received by the French Administration in Lome where it had been arranged for Botsio to deliver a personal message to Sylvanus Olympio. Grunitzky was then working in close collaboration with the French authorities to bring about the integration of Togoland in the French Union. Olympio was unpopular with the French because he was known to be opposed to this policy. He sought an independent Togo which would be linked with elements of the Ewe-speaking people on the Gold Coast–Togoland frontier. In Paris and in Rome our delegation called briefly on the British Ambassadors. In Bombay Botsio called on Morarji Desai, then a Minister in Nehru's government. There was general discussion of the Gold Coast and its expectation of independence. In Singapore Malcolm MacDonald, British Representative in Southeast Asia, who was our host, arranged for us to see new housing estates and to visit the House of Assembly. Here we met David Marshall, the Prime Minister, and Lee Kuan Yew, at that time already well-known as a brilliant lawyer and Leader of the Opposition. When we arrived in Bandung the third member of our delegation, Jimmie Markham, who had preceded us, was in hospital with cholera and had lost much weight with prolonged dehydration. However, he recovered in time to attend the Conference.

Botsio's address to the opening session had to take account of the Colonial Office warning about our status as observers and, at the same time, express the interest of our government in the anti-colonial struggle. I prepared a draft address, approved by Botsio, which showed our appreciation of the efforts of the Afro-Asian states in the anti-colonial struggle and expressed the hope that the Gold Coast and other African countries would be able to make their contribution on attaining independence. We managed to avoid the temptation to condemn colonialism. The address was warmly applauded. But, in spite of the applause, other leaders noted the cautious tone of Botsio's speech. W. Scott Thompson has recorded that Mohammed A. K. Hassouna submitted a report on the Bandung Conference to the Arab League in Cairo in which he described the Gold Coast as 'a follower of Britain'.[17] In the circumstances even this description was preferable to endangering the national interest of the Gold Coast by rashness.

The programme of decolonization pursued by Nkrumah after Bandung can only be understood in the general context of his African interests. But in the development of the diplomatic service, the important question to be examined is the extent to which career civil servants were prepared to accept unorthodox methods in the furtherance of this programme. Alex Quaison-Sackey, when he became Foreign

Minister in 1965 after a diplomatic career, raised the general question of reappraising not the objectives of the policy but the methods and procedures employed. This drew attention to an obvious paradox: a principal motive for expanding Ghana's representation abroad, providing an extensive career system, rested on a programme which career diplomats wished to control in a different way from that envisaged by the President. The general issue of the use of 'activists' in foreign, not diplomatic, service is further discussed later in this study.

GROWTH AND EXPANSION OF THE MINISTRY OF FOREIGN AFFAIRS

One of the most important missions was that to the UN. Ghana also established diplomatic relations with the USA, France, Liberia, and Israel* in 1957-8. By virtue of Ghana's membership of the Commonwealth, the government approved the setting up of High Commissions in London, New Delhi, Ottawa, and Canberra. In London the new High Commission absorbed the nucleus of a trade department which had been running under a Trade Commissioner. Another United Nations Mission was established in Geneva to deal with various UN bodies there. By the end of 1965 there were over sixty missions. The military regime after 1966 drastically reduced this number.

It was the responsibility of a Permanent Mission to provide Ghanaian representation for the various meetings of United Nations bodies that take place at the United Nations or in Geneva. It also provided staff for servicing home-based delegations that attended the international meetings in these areas from time to time. Officials of a Permanent Mission were not strictly regarded as accredited (or official representa-

* It is not surprising that Ghana should have included Liberia among the first diplomatic posts. The oldest independent state in West Africa, it had never been colonized by any European power. It may also be noted that with the growing prospect of Gold Coast independence, the friendship between Nkrumah and Padmore, developed at the 1945 Pan-African Congress, had deepened. Padmore's long-standing interest in Liberia, dating back to his student days in Howard University, was well known. With regard to Ghana's relations with Israel, which had been rather close from the eve of independence, one can detect Padmore's active influence. As a convinced Marxist he would have been sufficiently attracted by Israel's socialist programme of development, in spite of his knowledge that Israeli socialism left much to be desired. It is also doubtful whether Israel's Zionist austerity had been sufficiently appreciated in Ghana. See R. Hooker, *Black Revolutionary* (New York, 1967), pp. 12 and 135. It should be pointed out, however, that Hooker is wrong to relate Padmore's influence at this time to the Flagstaff House period of Nkrumah's regime. Nkrumah did not have use of that official residence until after the Governor-General, Listowel, left Ghana as part of the constitutional changes resulting from Ghana becoming a Republic within the Commonwealth in July 1960. Padmore died in 1959.

tives of Ghana) to the country where they were posted. Thus the Ghanaian representative at the United Nations did not normally provide diplomatic representation in the United States. Such representation, as well as information duties, was undertaken by the Ambassador in Washington. It was he who had accreditation to the White House. There was in addition a separate office in New York headed by a Consul-General who undertook consular duties.

Why did Nkrumah maintain so many missions abroad? Did he fail to count the cost? These questions cannot be answered in such a brief study. However, some clues may be sought from the political reasons for diplomatic representation and from conditions prevailing in Ghana after independence. The first reason for establishing diplomatic relations is to secure information from the outside world which it is in the national interest to possess. The best means of obtaining this is by the use of citizens of one's own country. As the interest of one country in another grows, so does the need to establish diplomatic links between them. Other things being equal, the more such links are made, the greater is the opportunity of serving the national interest. It appears that Nkrumah was prepared to pay any price in pursuit of this motive.

The second reason for the rapid growth of Ghana's Foreign Service is that it followed the general trend in the expansion of post-independence Ghana, particularly during the period 1958–64. During most of the period the gross national product per head in Ghana was the highest in Africa, with the exception of Libya and South Africa. This was, of course, before the discovery of oil in Libya and Nigeria. There was no lack of investment in her industries; there was growing evidence of modernization and industrialization—new roads, factories, hospitals and schools, harbours, the new township of Tema, the Volta and Tefle bridges, and the Volta Dam. Walter Birmingham and others have claimed that by 1960 the capital stock of Ghana stood at £175 per head of the population.[18]

An examination of Ghana's rate of expenditure shows that the Foreign Office was closely following the general trend in the country. Between 1951 and 1956 the Gold Coast, while still a colonial territory, had spent only £710,850 on the Ministry of Defence and External Affairs in preparation for independence. The scale of expenditure in the Foreign Service has been justly criticized as excessive. Nkrumah himself made repeated attempts to cut it down but the canker had eaten too deeply into the system to make any extensive reversal practicable. For example, the Ghanaian mission in the Sudan was at one time paying rent of £400 a month for office and residential accommodation. The original plan drawn up in 1959 to phase the expansion of Ghana's diplomatic representation was naturally not adhered to. The estimates for 1960–61 made provision for twenty-two embassies, and plans were laid to double this number in the following year. By June 1962 Ghana had forty-four embassies in operation with another nine in prospect, more than those of Australia.[19] The development of a process of administration involving parallel agencies came at a moment when the system of official representation was expanding at a prodigious rate. In Chapter 3 this peculiar development is considered.

3

SECRETARIAT EXPERIENCE

THE ORIGIN OF THE SECRETARIAT

In the course of 1960 the need for a 'new style' Secretariat machinery for dealing with Ghana's increasing responsibilities in Africa became apparent to Nkrumah. The independence of the Congo (now Zaire) had brought a new crisis of confidence which threatened to divide the independent African states into opposing groups. Nkrumah needed a body outside the Ministry to carry out his plans for arresting deterioration in the Congo crisis. A special Congo coordinating committee was set up under the chairmanship of Kwaku Boateng, the Minister of Information. Other members were Eric Otoo, who subsequently became head of the Special Intelligence Service, Geoffrey Bing, then Attorney-General, Major-General H. E. Alexander, and a military officer with the rank of Major who was an expert on logistics. Richard Quarshie, at the time my deputy, was appointed Secretary to the committee. I was also released from routine work as Principal Secretary of the Ministry to assist the setting up of a new Ghana Office in the Congo and to serve as administrative liaison between Nkrumah and Lumumba. In this way the Foreign Ministry was not only partially dismembered but also immobilized and virtually deprived of the opportunity of direct participation in the problems of the Congo.

The Congo experience convinced Nkrumah of the need to intensify his diplomatic activities for bringing the Casablanca and Monrovia powers more closely together. His aim was to carry out a two-pronged assault with the African Affairs Secretariat as his diplomatic arm and the Bureau of African Affairs as the chief instrument for promoting the liberation struggle in Africa.

He began a series of consultations with the heads of the independent African states to secure their agreement to the idea of continental unity. He considered that the same energy with which the colonial peoples had secured independence could be used for this and he also saw it as the surest foundation for economic stability; he had no doubt that 'a large geographical area contained within one political framework' would make for 'more rational economic planning'.[20]

The Secretariat was set up in April 1961 as a separate entity under the personal control of the President. It was formed from a small division in the Foreign Office which had previously dealt with all matters relating to Africa, and which had maintained some liaison before 1959 with George Padmore's office which dealt with the liberation of the dependent territories in Africa. This division thus became one of the Secretariats* in Flagstaff House together with others such as Fuel and Power, State Enterprises, Publicity, etc.

* In view of the speculation that has surrounded the formation of the Bureau of African Affairs, the African Affairs Secretariat, and the Congo Coordinating Committee, I have been glad to note a statement on the origins of these bodies prepared by K. B. Asante. As I indicate in subsequent paragraphs of this study, Asante was for many years my closest associate in Flagstaff House. His first-hand knowledge of the circumstances leading to the establishment of the organs mentioned are welcome for the record. Here is his comment:
'The origin of the Secretariat can be traced to the death of George Padmore. There was no one immediately available to take over the role of Padmore. Nkrumah therefore requested Ako Adjei to look into the possible modification and implementation of the instrument which established the Bureau.
'Ako Adjei suggested that the Director of the then Africa and UN Department, K. B. Asante, should take over the administration of the Bureau of African Affairs. In fact, the Director discussed the take-over with Mr A. K. Barden and actually established an office in the Bureau. Very shortly afterwards, he was sent to New York as a member of the Ghana delegation to the United Nations.
'This took place between July and September 1960. When he left for New York, Mr Ako Adjei, perhaps to thwart manoeuvres to alter the situation, requested the Acting Director, Mr Owusu Ansah, to move into the Bureau of African Affairs. By the time the Director returned from the UN, however, Mr Bosumtwi-Sam had been firmly installed in the Bureau of African Affairs as Secretary with Barden himself as Director. The attempt therefore to create a Secretariat cum Bureau failed.
'The Congo Committee was created as an ad hoc committee or an ad hoc body to deal with a crisis. Those who should normally be represented were on it. The Committee therefore started as an orthodox committee within the Foreign Ministry to deal with a specific situation under Nkrumah's supervision.
'The first instance of Nkrumah actually inviting a Foreign Service Officer for work on African Affairs in Flagstaff House was in January 1961 after the Casablanca Conference when he, Nkrumah, was charged with responsibility for implementing the decisions of the Conference. The Director of the African and UN Division of the Foreign Ministry was then given an office in Flagstaff House to deal with this implementation directly under Nkrumah. After completing this, he left for the Foreign Ministry only to be summoned back by Nkrumah.
'Later, upon the departure of Mr A. L. Adu for work outside the country, the Principal Secretary of the Ministry of Foreign Affairs, Mr Dei-Anang, was called to Flagstaff House, requested to sit in Adu's chair and work on African Affairs. Even Richard Akwei who was, after Dei-Anang's departure, in charge of the Foreign Ministry, was also given an office in Flagstaff House, but he managed to escape and went back to the Foreign Ministry. Shortly after Dei-Anang was installed in Flagstaff House came the Dawn Broadcast when Nkrumah announced the intention to create a Ministry of African Affairs. This never materialized, but the African Affairs Secretariat was established without any formal instrument. It eventually took charge of all aspects of representation in Africa.'

My colleagues were K. B. Asante, who subsequently became Principal Secretary of the Secretariat, and E. P. Seddoh, head of Administration, Personnel and Accounts. 'KB', as he came to be known in official circles, was a most effective aide; he was intelligent, active, and possessed abundant capacity for work. We often wondered how one with such a small physique came to generate so much energy. Seddoh was invaluable in our relations with the French-speaking African states, as he spoke English and French with equal facility, having completed his university education at the Sorbonne. Added to this was his extensive knowledge of Francophone Africa and its leading political representatives. When the work of the Secretariat had become fairly well established, we tried to get him appointed an Ambassador to one of these states. But our efforts were unavailing, since his candidature was turned down in favour of political appointees.

Our team was strengthened by the addition of H. A. Amonoo of the Foreign Office. His knowledge of United Nations procedures and capacity for 'lobbying' made him an excellent associate. Small though the Secretariat was initially, all its members, even subordinate personnel, tried to make up for numbers by the quality of their work. Office accommodation was limited as this was allocated to us by the Cabinet Office which had to share its own office space with us at short notice. Whatever was required at any moment of time, the Secretariat tried to provide readily. If long and sustained loads of work had any pernicious effect on the human system, none of us would have survived. One of us actually managed to put on considerable weight despite this, and once attracted Nkrumah's notice. He pointed to his bulging tummy when he passed a group of us, told him jokingly he was growing 'prematurely prosperous', and then proceeded to show us how he kept his own weight down by a systematic course of Yoga exercises!

BUREAU OF AFRICAN AFFAIRS

George Padmore had gone to Ghana as Nkrumah's adviser on African affairs. His death was not allowed to interrupt that work. His Office was converted into the Bureau of African Affairs with Nkrumah as its Director. A. K. Barden, ex-serviceman and Padmore's stenographer, was appointed Secretary.[21] On 4 May 1960 it was

---

It is perhaps necessary to add that the African Affairs Centre, located in the airport residential area on Dodowa Road, very close to the Airport roundabout, provided hostel facilities for Freedom Fighters. Initially it was run under the auspices of the Bureau; but Nkrumah pragmatically resolved growing conflict between Barden and T. R. Makonnen, who was in charge, as he always did in cases of such personal strains around him, by making Makonnen accountable to himself through the African Affairs Secretariat.

officially announced that the Bureau had been established by statutory instrument and given formal and independent existence as a Statutory Board. A new board of directors was appointed: Tawia Adamafio, Andrew Yaw K. Djin, Peter Mbiyu Koinange, T. R. Makonnen, John Tettegah, and Nathaniel A. Welbeck (Chairman).

It appears from its subsequent history that a change of control led to a change of direction and emphasis. First, the Board members had full-time responsibilities elsewhere; this did not permit them to direct the affairs of the Bureau as carefully as was necessary. Second, Nkrumah ceased to be Director and appointed Barden to replace him. Barden was directly answerable to Nkrumah. In these circumstances, the members failed to show active interest in its work. The links which were intended to be maintained with the Foreign Ministry, never actually strong, were completely dissolved. The main functions of the Bureau included provision of assistance to freedom fighters in the remaining colonial territories of Africa and the provision of training for political elements from these territories as well as funds to enable leaders from those areas to keep up their struggle. The Bureau was also expected to provide hostel facilities for freedom fighters who fled from their countries for political reasons. Ghana's anti-colonial policy drew large numbers to Accra. Among these were a number of opposition politicians seeking asylum in Ghana from certain independent African states, including the so-called Kingdom of Sanwi (in the Ivory Coast), the Cameroons, and Niger.

Neither the Foreign Office nor the African Affairs Secretariat had any direct responsibility for these elements other than that of ensuring that they were properly housed and fed. Some of them, such as S. G. Ikoku of Nigeria, were engaged in gainful employment on the understanding that they would refrain from political activities which could embarrass the government of Ghana. Ikoku was a brilliant economist and was employed in the Kwame Nkrumah Ideological School in Winneba and on the editorial staff of *Spark*.

There is no doubt, however, that Nkrumah used the presence of political refugees for bargaining purposes with the other African leaders. He often said that his security and intelligence services provided him with detailed accounts of the activities of certain Ghanaian exiles in other territories and believed that these activities were known to, if not actively supported by, the political leaders of those states. It must be said however that the presence of these political refugees in Ghana did much to destroy harmonious relations between Ghana and other African states, hampering Nkrumah's work for African unity. The 1965 OAU Conference in Ghana was almost wrecked by the refusal of some heads of government to attend unless certain of their citizens in Ghana whom they regarded as subversive were expelled. Prominent among the protesting heads of state were Sir Abubakar Tafawa Balewa of Nigeria, President Hamani Diori of Niger, and President Houphouet-Boigny of the Ivory Coast. Politically, Nkrumah did not attach great importance to the affair, pointing out that, as long as these states encouraged Ghanaian opposition elements to exercise their hostility towards Ghana from their territories, they were being hypocritical in denouncing Ghana's hospitality to their exiles. He also felt that some of these states were using their denunciation of subversion as a cover for their neo-colonialist links with foreign powers.

FRICTION BETWEEN AGENCIES

It was impossible to operate the parallel organizations of the Foreign Ministry, African Affairs Secretariat, and the Bureau of African Affairs without causing some disharmony in relations. The main friction was between the Ministry of Foreign Affairs and the African Affairs Secretariat. Since the Ministry was some distance from the office of the President, it was not always possible to associate the Foreign Minister with urgent discussions on African issues initiated by the President. If an African ambassador called on the President, a note of the discussions that took place would be prepared by a senior official of the African Affairs Secretariat; in these circumstances, the Secretariat had access to such information before it reached the Minister. The Minister was therefore often one step behind in the despatch of official business. Although notes prepared on such occasions were submitted to the Minister as rapidly as possible, even a short time lag could embarrass him, if he happened to meet the particular ambassador before a note of that discussion had reached him. On other occasions, where a note was not available and the Minister had not yet had occasion to meet the President, it became necessary for him to be briefed by officials of the Secretariat, a situation which was not always pleasant for either party. Since the Minister was Ghana's representative at international meetings and was expected to be fully informed about developments in Ghana's African policy, the whole situation was altogether unsatisfactory. Ako Adjei, the longest serving Foreign Minister (1959–62), who was dismissed after the Kulungugu attempt on the President's life, was greatly reduced in influence by the autumn of 1961.

Another source of friction was duplication of effort as between the Ministry and the Secretariat, separate divisions of protocol, accounts, personnel, etc. being maintained in each organization. Apart from the obvious fact that this did not make for the most efficient use of available resources, some of the best officials in the Ministry felt themselves 'left out' as their talents did not have full scope for development.

As the liberation struggle in Africa gained momentum, further friction developed. Within the Bureau there was the tendency to adopt the unorthodox line of diplomacy which invariably provoked foreign governments. Since it was entrusted with responsibility for the guerilla training of freedom fighters, other governments in Africa, particularly those in neighbouring territories, saw Ghana as the source of most of their domestic difficulties. A stage was even reached where certain diplomatic representatives were selected by the President from the 'activists' operating within the Bureau. From these sources of friction developed the checks on the operations of the Ministry of Foreign Affairs and the African Affairs Secretariat which, as time went by, diminished much of the value of the work done by Ghana for Africa. Examples of the development of such friction are referred to later in this study.

The crisis of confidence created by this situation did not appear to worry Nkrumah. Most foreign service officers wanted the Secretariat abolished and expressed this view at a conference of diplomats, officials of the Ministry, and the Secretariat in January 1962. However, in the mind of Nkrumah, the Foreign Ministry was identified with a slow, inactive, and orthodox service incapable of reacting effectively to his needs. Nkrumah was a man in a hurry, and, in his view, the business of Africa could not wait. Action and more action were his first imperatives at all times, and speed in achieving this was of paramount importance to him. Although his hurry did not in my experience reduce his willingness to listen to disagreement, he was definitely impatient with it. This often caused him to forget the well-known Akan saying 'Okwan tia ye mmusu' (a short cut is a disastrous route). Diplomatic work is sometimes a slow business, requiring patience, considerable tact, and caution and even when operated by experienced staff its results are not always spectacular or immediate.

The activities of the Bureau continued to loom large in African affairs. A. K. Barden undertook great risks in perilous journeys under various guises throughout Africa. On these missions he conveyed Nkrumah's directives, medical supplies, and anti-colonial documents to freedom fighters. Confidence in Barden stemmed from Nkrumah's respect for his willingness to respond at all times to the many demands that were made on his courage and loyalty in the liberation cause. Later, not very long before the break-up of the regime, the Nkrumah–Barden relationship seems to have suffered some kind of breach, the background of which was undisclosed.

CONSEQUENCES OF THE SECRETARIAT SYSTEM

The President became almost the sole initiator of policy, and it was impossible for administrators to argue demarcation of responsibilities which would have restricted any particular agency to an agreed role. Barden carried out the President's personal instructions which were not conveyed to other parts of the civil service machine. Scott Thompson has argued that Nkrumah never formally adopted 'intervention' in independent Africa as a tool of policy, and that the broadening use of subversive techniques came in large measure by accident.[22] A system of government agencies with very limited coordination provided the environment for creating flexibility in the definition of policy. This may not be sound administrative practice but it gave Nkrumah the flexibility he needed for dealing with political situations in a fast growing state. It would be a mistake to suppose that the Secretariat system retained any of the basic features of cabinet government. The system was a kind of 'marriage of convenience' between the civil service and Nkrumah who, after the disruption of confidence between himself and most of his Ministers resulting from the Kulungugu assassination attempt, found no means of carrying on an effective cabinet system of administration.

At the height of the President's reliance on a series of secretariat offices (1962–3), there were twelve Secretariats at Flagstaff House and twelves Ministries on a separate 'campus' in Accra. The subjects for which the President was directly responsible were assigned to over twenty separate departments. The principal Secretariats were Cabinet, Establishment, State Functions, Scholarships, African Affairs, Organization and Methods, Fuel and Power, Architectural and Engineering, and Publicity.[23] Government was therefore divided into presidential subjects and ministerial subjects. Any subject over which the President wanted immediate control came into the Secretariat system. It is beyond the scope of this study to estimate the relative influence on policy formulation of different parts of the government machine, but it is important to stress how they all revolved round the President himself. After 1961 individual Ministers carried very little weight.[24] In this study, I attempt to show what it was like to operate.

In my job I was constantly required to confirm with the President that he had instructed Barden to undertake certain activities in independent Africa about which I had heard from other sources. The Bureau had its own organization but was also able to use the orthodox diplomatic channels. For example, the Bureau often worked through a member of one of the established missions in Africa, who would be permitted to use the wireless transmitter but employed a separate code for communication with his headquarters. The Bureau was also able to use the diplomatic bag for the transmission of messages and supplies, but under a separate seal. The Foreign Office was thus not always in a position to censor communication between Barden and his field associates. In this situation there was no one major system for reporting events in Africa. The 'orthodox diplomatic channels' outside Africa were affected by the many different kinds of access to his ear which the President allowed. Ambassadors were by no means all equal in status and influence. Their effectiveness and influence were largely determined by the usefulness and propriety of the advice which they were able to tender to the President. After 1961 ambassadors in the African field were regarded as no longer under the administrative control of the Foreign Ministry. Their reports ceased to go direct to the Foreign Minister, as their new chain of authority lay through the Secretariat to the President, who thus became their new head of department. Where necessary, some of their reports were copied to the Foreign Ministry and the Secretariat. I was at the butt end of the odium this created.

It is not surprising that the morale of the diplomatic service was gravely damaged. As already indicated, the tension between my own Secretariat and the Ministry was particularly obvious at the meeting of envoys in January 1962. Many speakers strongly advocated the disbanding of the Secretariat; some even implied that I sought to maintain the separate existence of the Secretariat in my own interests. It was not generally known that on administrative grounds I was opposed to separate existence, while Nkrumah himself was quite equivocal on the issue.* He explained that he did not wish to see African affairs go outside his control. He did not believe that any other Minister could handle urgent African problems as well as he could. None of his Ministers disputed this view or called it in question.

The other Secretariat which played an increasing role in diplomatic affairs was that concerned with publicity. It was a particularly effective medium for arranging propaganda handouts, launching the President's own publications, and the general dissemination of news about government policies, to the foreign press. It was far more effective for these purposes than the Ministry of Information. The Secretariats held

---

* K. B. Asante's comment on this point is interesting: 'Nkrumah was equivocal. In fact, at one time, he requested Botsio who was the Foreign Minister to arrange for the merger of the Secretariat and the Foreign Ministry. Such incidents led to the belief that it was the senior officials of the Secretariat who prevailed upon President Nkrumah against his wishes to maintain the separate existence of the Secretariat. Nkrumah made it quite clear to the senior officials of the Secretariat that to him the Foreign Ministry did not exist. He even stated once that the Foreign Ministry should be burned down. Perhaps for reasons of tact or politics, he never made this clear to the Minister or officials of the Foreign Ministry.'

Monday morning conferences with representatives of the press corps and with the President's publicity advisers in order to decide what line to project. On particular occasions, official pronouncements were discussed at these meetings in a draft form.

As far as African Affairs were concerned, the most influential section of the press corps and the most important group of collaborators were those associated with *The Spark*, which was founded in December 1962. The President used this paper to try out ideas and to put forward policies which could not be disseminated through orthodox channels. Reactions to the newspaper in other independent African countries sometimes led to serious diplomatic embarrassment. One example of this is probably sufficient here. On the day the 1964 OAU Conference was taking place in Cairo, the French version of *Spark*, *L'Etincelle*, put out an issue, circulated at the Conference, which actually referred to some of the heads of state present in terms which were neither flattering nor commendatory. One of them was described as a 'neo-colonialist'!

As an administrator, I had to design an office which was capable of meeting the demands placed on it. Although a great deal of formal coordination was in the hands of the President, I took pains to ensure that the Ministry was as adequately informed as possible. My own Secretariat gained immeasurably in its effectiveness from its location. As in the case of the location of other Secretariats under his control, this was, in my view, one of Nkrumah's main purposes in its establishment.

NKRUMAH'S METHODS OF WORK

Nkrumah attended to official business with care and concern above the ordinary. He was a stickler for discipline and hated lazy, slipshod, or slovenly work of any kind. Nor did he stint himself of work. His working day started long before day-break with reading the day's papers, and a 'pet' book—usually a biography, such as Mazzini, Machiavelli, Dante, Freud, Madame Curie, Napoleon, the Duke of Wellington, or Lenin. He was a most avid reader, covering practically every discipline under the sun—history, politics, science, economics, from which he was quick to draw the main substance with apparent ease. I know this, because in relaxed moments he would sometimes pass on a book which he had just finished reading with the casual remark—'Dei, see how you like this book—I found it interesting'.[25] One characteristic note in a book he had just read said about the word, *neo-colonialism*, 'that phrase was coined by me', meaning himself.[26] He was always punctual at the office, and was at work all day with interviews with ministers, diplomats, senior officials, party representatives, chiefs, clergymen, professors, businessmen (Sir Edward Spears of Ashanti Goldfields Ltd. and Chad Calhoun, the Vice-President of Kaiser Industries, were frequent callers), police and army 'top brass', foreign dignitaries, pressmen, market-women, and as many little-known personages as could get their names in his official interview list either by meeting him personally somewhere or by appointment with the Cabinet Office and Security Staff. The procedure for securing an interview was not complicated or difficult, if one knew it.[27] It was to telephone or call on either the President's Security Chief, the Cabinet Secretary, or his Deputy to ask for an appointment. A few top-ranking party representatives and VIPs who had his private telephone number could telephone direct for an appointment. Ambassadors and high commissioners, both Ghanaian and foreign, normally made calls on the President either through the Minister of Foreign Affairs or through the African Affairs Secretariat.

The question of ambassadors' access to the President has often been regarded as a reliable barometer of the President's political prejudices or leanings. There was the widespread belief that the Soviet Ambassador in Ghana, Georgi Rodionov, had Nkrumah's ear above every other diplomat, and from this the inference was drawn that the President was leaning too heavily on the Soviet Government. But this is only a superficial assessment. Nkrumah had plenty of time for any one who either had anything worthwhile to tell him or was ready to provide help when urgently needed. Like Huang Hua of the People's Republic of China, who was a much respected member of the Communist hierarchy in Peking, Rodionov was a top-ranking party man in the Soviet Union before his assignment to Ghana. He was thus a man of considerable experience. The President knew this, and took much advantage of it. The timing of this warm relationship between Rodionov and Nkrumah was also significant—the West had apparently lost its positive interest in Ghana, for their representatives were generally inexperienced or second-rate non-career diplomats or appointees with no settled ideological or political convictions.

For example, the American Ambassador, Franklyn Williams, although an Afro-American and a former Lincolnian, like Nkrumah, was not a career diplomat and was also unhappily suspected by Nkrumah of CIA connections. Against this background, it is important to recall that William Mahoney, Williams' predecessor, was a warm and experienced Roman Catholic lawyer, believed to be a personal friend of Kennedy. He had easy access to Nkrumah at all times; some of his children (he had eleven) were even at school in Flagstaff House with the President's and other Ghanaian children.

Phone calls to the President's Office were generally efficient, the operators being carefully selected for courtesy, experience, intelligence, and sense of responsibility. Hitches that occurred during phone calls to the Office were due mainly to a breakdown in the main Post Office. In view of the general belief that every corner of Nkrumah's Office was 'bugged', it may be of interest to state that he did not even have scrambler telephones. On one occasion I was in his Office when the phone rang. An apparently saucy exchange operator enquired rudely 'Who are you?' Such was the man's sense of humour that he burst out laughing and said to me, 'Dei, you answer.' I answered the girl, 'You were speaking to the President's Office.' One could almost hear the telephone receiver drop at the other end. However, after the Kulungugu assassination attempt in 1962, it became more difficult for casual visitors to get past the Security Office.

In the office he scrutinized every file with the greatest attention to detail. He would not accept any assignment as complete unless every form of consultation necessary had been carried out. In spite of the fact that he made considerable work for himself by insisting on examining personally every problem of Ghana's development, finance, and administration as well as matters concerning political issues and educational and medical services, his desk was never marked by unfinished files. Indeed, in all my experience of work under him, I cannot recollect ever seeing that huge pile of unattended files usually found in some busy offices. He hated like poison the 'pending' tray, regarding it as an excuse for laziness; he said it was inconsiderate of any officer to keep any subject on the 'pending' list, since official work concerned the welfare of Ghanaian taxpayers.*

Although he enjoyed a good meal, he was not a 'glutton' or a 'wine-bibber'. His main drink was always 'soft', although he was not averse to champagne on ceremonial occasions. He believed that corpulence was the result of over-eating, laziness, and lack of discipline and often poked fun at an official or politician who was putting on undue weight as 'prosperous' or 'decadent'. Friday was his fast day; he would touch no food until after 6 p.m., when he broke his fast with a glass of lemon water. And yet Friday was, strangely enough, his longest

---

* On this point A. L. Adu has also pointed out that in his view it would be 'fair and correct to add that Nkrumah had a genius for selecting highly competent officers for his headquarters staff who ensured that all matters which were to be presented to him had been pre-digested and properly examined in the light of his known policies, attitude, and approach. This made his task of working on his files comparatively easy.' In the light of this statement, from one of the most experienced members of the Ghanaian civil service, Nkrumah's official staff could be regarded rather as technocrats or 'think-tanks' than the pliable 'sycophants' or ambitious 'climbers' they were generally given out to be at the time of his overthrow.

working day—when he would go on working with you without regard to the lunch hour. Officials working close to him soon became aware of this; he was not deliberately depriving others of their lunch, it was simply out of his thoughts on Friday! In spite of all this, he was a most genial boss and showed considerable attachment to anyone who proved to be a steady and conscientious worker. He often had snacks such as chocolates, sandwiches, and tea or soft drinks served to break the pressure and strain of arduous work.

He was a man of equable temperament. Like all heads of state, he had his emotional outbursts; he was also a pastmaster in the art of simulating carefully delivered anger. To those who were aware of the use of these masks, he would subsequently break out in child-like laughter, ending up with 'I have to do that occasionally for the sake of Ghana! Some people need this kind of dose now and again.'

A TYPICAL DAY

To provide some idea of the nature of work in the Secretariat, I describe below what may be regarded as a normal day in my own office.

My morning began in the Office at 7.30, by which time the President was already at his desk. In my in-tray minutes which had been submitted to him the previous day had been returned for attention. My stenographer/secretary, a young Ghanaian girl who was bilingual in French and English, would have put up my daily diary as follows:

9 a.m.   Meeting with representatives of Ministries of Trade, Finance, Agriculture, and Trade Manager of the Ghana National Trading Corporation on supply of meat from Mali.
10 a.m. Ghana's High Commissioner, Nigeria.
11 a.m. Upper Volta Delegation.
12 noon Meet OAU Secretary-General at airport.
2 p.m.   State Publishing Corporation Meeting.
5 p.m.   Senegal Ambassador calls.
6.30 p.m. Independence Anniversary of Liberia. Drinks party at Ambassador Hotel.

Before the day's programme started, the President's files had to be glanced through quickly to see whether he wanted to raise any urgent matters from the previous day's minutes during the course of the morning. Thereafter, the morning's letters had to be reviewed rapidly for any matters which might require attention by telex or telephone.

In the course of these hurried surveys, the intercom system buzzed.

I was No. 1, and therefore this indicated a call from the President. 'Dei-Anang, one minute, please.' When one arrived it really was little more than a minute. He had 'heard' that an Upper Volta delegation was in the country. Were we expecting them? Indeed, we weren't. They sent a special message through their embassy only yesterday to notify us of their coming. Neither our Office in Ouagadougou nor the Secretariat had been warned of their intentions. But they would be received by the senior French-speaking official, since the delegation was at low official level; a report would be made in the course of the day.

K. B. Asante, my Deputy, and I then held a quick meeting on the day's work. He had his own files to account for, of course, ranging from preparation of summaries of reports, internal disciplinary problems, transfers, increments, incoming mail from African missions, etc. Anyhow, could he join me at 10 to receive the High Commissioner from Nigeria? He was also to ask Patrick Seddoh to meet the Upper Volta Delegation and prepare notes of their discussion. He should not hesitate to call on either of us to participate, if necessary.

Harry Amonoo, in charge of protocol and the African schedule, should be reminded to accompany me to the airport at noon to meet the OAU Secretary-General. He should check that a car had been provided for his two-day stay, as well as accommodation at the Government Hospitality Centre (This housing facility was more conducive to privacy, and cost far less than accommodation in a hotel.). A minute on his visit was among the papers submitted by our Office to the President the previous day and Harry was to make an appointment for him to call on the President next day.

KB attended the Trade Meeting at 9 in order to free me to attend to Mr Tay, Ghana's High Commissioner in Nigeria, at 10; he was to join me when that meeting was over. The points to stress at the trade meeting were as follows:

(i) as part of our commercial exchanges with Mali, the Mali authorities had agreed to supply x tons of carcases per week. Clear with Ministry of Trade;

(ii) The GNTC was to arrange transportation through Ghana Airways. This had to be cleared with 'Communications';

(iii) A major factor in these transactions was the eventual supply of Ndama cattle to be reared in suitable areas of Ghana's Northern and Upper Regions. When established, these stocks were expected to supply a base for 'feeding' the new corned beef factory in Bolgatanga, in the Upper Region. Papers on these proposals had been submitted to the Ministry of Agriculture and the Department of Animal Husbandry for study.

At 10 Mr Tay came in to say that he was on a routine call prior to resuming duty in Lagos after a period of leave. There was no urgent business (Asante need not attend), but he was being asked to consider proposals for opening sub-offices in the regional centres of Nigeria on which he must submit a report. He was also to be supplied with copies of Publicity Secretariat documents and publications on inter-African relations and continental union for distribution. Since my records showed that he had seen the President when he arrived from Lagos there was no special need to call on him before his return.

Meanwhile, my secretary came in to say that there was a call from the African Centre. The Sanwi refugees of the Ivory Coast wanted an appointment made for them to see 'Osagyefo'. The secretary was instructed to request 'King' Ammon Ndoufou, Atie, and Bile alone to come and talk to us, to enable us to prepare the necessary papers which must be submitted to the President before their call on him. This was always a good 'screening' device enabling us to sort out inessential matters and take some of the load off the President. As the meeting with the Ghana High Commissioner did not consume much time, I could receive the refugees between 10.30 and 12 noon. The Sanwi leaders were a dissident faction from the Ivory Coast who claimed 'sovereignty' outside the Ivory Coast government. This claim had no constitutional basis: they had therefore fled and sought refuge in Ghana where Nkrumah undertook to seek a settlement on their behalf with President Houphouet-Boigny. But they were not silent or politically discreet guests: they often embarrassed the government by making fantastic claims for their sovereignty in published documents to which they gave extensive publicity in and out of Ghana. Everything possible was done officially to restrain them but with indifferent success. The Secretariat therefore proposed that they should be accommodated in a settlement in the forest area of Western Ghana where they could sustain themselves in their traditional vocations as farmers and fishermen. Nana Kobina Nketsia was appointed to organize this settlement complete with farmsteads and bungalows in a timber estate (Hiawa in the Western Region) abandoned by a commercial firm. It was thought that this would take their minds off political agitation and also remove them from urban influences in Accra. They were opposed to these proposals and wished to make their own case to the President. I assured them that their view of that matter would be put to the President who would then let them know his decision in due course. This was clearly not to their liking. The meeting of the Board of the State Publishing Corporation took place in my office at 2 p.m. and I presided as Chairman. Matters considered included the printing of school textbooks and stationery. After that meeting I had to settle down to an examination of the files in my tray which had to be attended to before the Senegal Ambassador called. At 5.30 p.m. Seddoh came along to give details of the discussions between him and the Upper Volta Delegation. A draft report to the President was left with me for submission.

I got home by 6.15 p.m. in time to change hurriedly for the Liberian independence anniversary party. The Liberian Ambassador was *doyen* of the Diplomatic Corps and a very close friend, two strong reasons compelling my attendance, in spite of the day's fatigue and my inherent distaste for diplomatic receptions.

4

POLICY PRACTICE IN AFRICA

CREATING A CONTINENTAL OUTLOOK

Visitors to my office in the Secretariat saw a large map of Africa specially produced by the survey division of the army, showing in one colour the states of Africa that had become independent since 1957 and those awaiting independence in a contrasting colour. As new states gained independence the map was brought up to date.

Before the establishment of the OAU, one of the most effective means of arousing a sense of unity and keeping up interest in the African liberation struggle was to ensure that Ghana's diplomatic representatives in the independent African states disseminated as widely as possible information on the extent to which Ghana was assisting freedom fighters in Angola, Mozambique, Guinea-Bissau, Rhodesia, and South West Africa. As Ghana was in no position to dictate policy to sister African states, it was found that the best practical course was to endeavour to lead by example. While no independent African state would brook any kind of interference from any quarter, the leaders of the new states were constantly looking over their shoulders to see what was happening elsewhere, and tried not to be outshone by any others within the limits of their own resources.[28] For example, it was known in Ghana that the UAR had a notable record for giving assistance to freedom fighters and that freedom fighters were greatly encouraged by Algeria after its independence. To stimulate interest in the liberation fronts, our representatives in these states sent frequent reports on the extent and nature of the help being given.

Another factor which aided the creation of a continental outlook, to which Nkrumah paid considerable attention, was the ability to make the world increasingly aware of an 'African presence' in international relations.[29] We began to cultivate this through the exchange of visits between friendly African states. Our ambassadors were instructed to discuss the nature of the visits proposed. For example, women's and youth organizations, where they existed in the states which had exchanged diplomatic representations with Ghana, were invited to send representatives to tour Ghana. Madame Gulama, then the only woman traditional Chief of Sierra Leone, made an official visit to

Ghana in 1964. In the following year, a team of Congolese women exchanged visits with a similar team from Ghana. How did the Secretariat select the team of Ghanaian women? The selection was normally made by the President himself from a list of candidates submitted to the Secretariat by the Secretary of the Council of Ghana Women, a wing of the CPP.

Even sport helped to highlight the African cause. Great emphasis was placed on Ghana's predominance in athletics to demonstrate Africa's readiness to acknowledge the development of the whole man as one of the factors in national growth. Inter-African games and football competitions were organized and Nkrumah provided an African Soccer Challenge Cup. The Ghanaian Sports Organizer was brought into close touch with developments in the Secretariat and when he travelled to any African state with his team he was carefully briefed in the Secretariat. Sometimes arrangements were made for the team to be received by the President before its departure.

Further point was given to the establishment of the African presence in the early 1960s when the East African territories became independent. Before the independence of these countries Ghana had developed close links with their leaders.[30] Mboya and Murumbi of Kenya and Nyerere of Tanganyika had been among those who had been specially invited to attend Ghana's first anniversary celebrations in March 1958. These contacts were further developed when these states became independent. Ghana sent two senior police officials to help Tanganyika with police organization and training. A senior Ghanaian legal officer was employed in the Tanzanian judiciary up to the time of the Ghana coup. For a number of years there were two Ghanaian Justices on the East African Court of Appeal with its headquarters in Nairobi[31] and the East African Common Services Organization was for some time headed by A. L. Adu, my own predecessor at the Ministry of Foreign Affairs. The first African legal draftsman in Uganda was V. C. R. A. Crabbe, posted on loan until a Ugandan national could be found to take the post.

DIPLOMATIC APPOINTMENTS

For dealing with the sensitive relationships with newly independent African states, it was vital that Ghana's diplomatic representatives should be extremely intelligent and circumspect. Nkrumah had decided that there should be a Ghanaian diplomat in every African state willing to exchange representatives. In the dependent territories Ghana endeavoured to station trained 'activists' who would keep in close touch with the freedom fighters and be a link between them and Nkrumah.

The Bureau of African Affairs with Barden as its Director provided training for these activists, Nkrumah himself giving the training his personal surveillance. Initially the selection of activist candidates was done on the basis of nominations to an African Affairs Committee over which Nkrumah presided. In the course of time, however, the Committee ceased to be active as the urgent demands of guerilla fighters made the summoning of meetings a relatively slow business. Much of the work of selecting candidates thus fell on Barden and Nkrumah. This created the impression, which Scott Thompson has described, that Barden had a free hand to appoint ambassadors for certain areas of Africa. It is impossible to think of Nkrumah abdicating his authority to Barden to such an extent.

In the case of independent African states the selection of diplomatic representatives was made by the Foreign Minister or the President. Whenever vacancies occurred the Secretariat put up career diplomats for consideration on the basis of seniority, proven ability, and experience but such nominations were invariably turned down in favour of politicians. It was only when an appointment required specialized skills, such as a knowledge of French, that nominations from the career stream secured a comparatively easy passage through the political network. Ben Placca and A. K. Foli were selected for appointment to Niger and Senegal respectively on this basis. E. M. Debrah, who was also selected from the career stream, proved to be particularly successful. He was subsequently Ambassador to Washington. The crowning point of these appointments was that of Alex Quaison-Sackey who, as already indicated, distinguished himself by becoming President of the UN General Assembly.

Reference has been made to the selection of 'activists' for special posting to dependent territories by the Bureau. In the course of time attempts to convert these 'activists' into diplomatic representatives in some of the independent African states raised problems examples of which must be mentioned here. In Mauretania, our relations, which had initially been quite good, diminished in importance and warmth. As far as Tanzania was concerned, there was an official protest against the conduct of the representative, who was considered indiscreet and almost hostile; a request for his removal was promptly satisfied. Another appointee from outside the diplomatic career stream was removed from Somalia owing to growing strain at his post.* A notable

* Scott Thompson refers to this situation rather uncritically in the particular case of relations between Dr Kaunda and Dr Nkrumah. It should be noted that Scott Thompson allowed himself to be greatly influenced by the hostility and prejudice against the Nkrumah regime naturally prevalent in post-coup Ghana. He took full advantage of this to produce a book which may have been sensational

exception was the appointment of David Busumtwi-Sam of the Bureau as Ghana's Ambassador in Uganda and then in Kenya. He was such a successful representative that his advice on East African problems was much valued by the Secretariat.

On the whole the appointment of politicians as ambassadors to African countries was a constant source of friction. Soon after independence nominations for such posts were made by the party executive of the CPP of which the Prime Minister was General Secretary. In due course the practice of making nominations fell to the President and the Foreign Minister as a general rule. In practice nominations for ambassadorial positions by officials, except within the normal career stream, were resented by politicians. This is perhaps understandable, since foreign representation was a popular means of rewarding party members for their loyalty and zeal.

SYSTEMATIC REPORTING

Much of the work of ambassadors was devoted to regular reporting from their missions to Accra. There were two main categories of reports. The first often went directly to the President, sometimes being copied to the Foreign Minister and officials. If the report was addressed to the President only, he often sent the papers down later, either through the Foreign Minister or direct to officials with specific instructions as to their disposal. At other times, he would only make a marginal note, such as 'See me'. The nature of the ensuing discussion would then indicate whether or not agreement was reached on the way in which the particular subject was to be dealt with. The President insisted on an

---

at the time of its appearance but in my view this situation detracted considerably from its scholarship and relevance. It is, for example, not accurate to say as he does on p.344 that 'not long after the Addis Ababa conference Nkrumah had given Barden sufficient power to put men in Ghanaian missions anywhere on the continent to circumvent the work of professional diplomats'. The correct position was that Nkrumah wanted 'activists' in all the dependent African territories to assist the nationalist leaders in their struggle against colonial occupation of their countries. This is work for which the selected candidates were specially trained, and not within the experience of diplomatic service personnel. In any case, without independent status, there was no room for diplomats or diplomatic work in those territories. Also, the selection and training of the activists was not the sole responsibility of Barden. It was done under the general supervision of Dr Nkrumah with the assistance of an African Affairs Committee consisting of party, Foreign Ministry, trade union, and African Affairs Secretariat representatives. Activists were trained specifically for direct involvement in the national aspirations of the dependent countries to which they were assigned. They were expected to provide some of the strategy for decolonization of their territories from guidelines prepared from CPP experience in pre-independent Ghana. In this sense, activists had a different orientation from that of diplomatic personnel.

acknowledgement being returned in respect of every report addressed to him, giving precise instructions or advice, or requesting further information on specific points. The second category of reports from field officers went direct to officials and usually concerned routine matters.* If no expenditure was called for by such reports, they were disposed of at the official level. Occasionally, a recommendation would involve expenditure for which no provision had been made in the Estimates, the subject being too urgent to be deferred to the following year, and in that event, and subject to the Minister's approval, a cabinet memorandum would be prepared to secure authority for the expenditure.

THE ADDIS ABABA CONFERENCE 1963

Throughout the last quarter of 1961 and early 1962 Nkrumah considered the basis for discussion among the independent African states in order to reach a decision on the creation of pan-African organizations. On 12 May 1962 he despatched a circular letter to the heads of state of independent African countries setting out his proposals for a common economic planning organization, a joint military command, and a common foreign policy system in a 'Union of African States'. He was accused of wishing to make Accra the capital of Africa. Before the Addis Ababa Conference of 1963 he sent a special two-man delegation, Kojo Botsio and Nana Kobina Nketsia, to the Central African Republic to ask whether the government of that country would consent to its capital being proposed as Africa's capital city. President Sekou Touré, President Modibo Keita, and others worked energetically to secure the support of the Emperor Haile Selassie and other leading African heads of state for summoning an All-African Conference in Ethiopia.

Kwesi Armah, then Ghana's High Commissioner in London, was allocated funds to organize a students' conference in Europe—embracing student bodies of French-speaking and English-speaking Africa—to stimulate support among youth for this new political idea. It was felt that such a conference would induce African intellectuals to bring pressure to bear on their own governments to express support for the

* It should perhaps be noted here that Ghanaian diplomats in the field complained consistently about the absence of a positive 'feedback' from the Foreign Ministry and subsequently, from the African Affairs Secretariat. This weakness underlines the absence of effective machinery at base for analysing and carrying out a systematic study of reports submitted. True, there were the usual 'area desks' where the problems of particular regions as they affected Ghana were given some attention. The missions had, however, expanded much faster than the organization at home, a situation which, in my experience, was never corrected.

idea of a pan-African government. At this time the leaders of most African states were unhappy about the existence of various political groupings, such as the Casablanca organization, the Monrovia group, and the Brazzaville group. If they did not share Nkrumah's conviction about unity, at least they understood that a coming-together of all the various groupings would assist in reconciling opposing views.

A few weeks before the Conference K. B. Asante was sent to Addis Ababa with a carefully selected team of officials to assist Ambassador E. M. Debrah with the arrangements for the Ghanaian delegation. Provision of suitable accommodation for delegations was always a constant source of irritation at conferences. Senior Ministers could not be doubled up—although officials invariably were. It was necessary to ensure that high-ranking party functionaries received similar consideration to Ministers in matters of accommodation and transport. In view of the fact that some thirty-two national delegations were expected in Addis Ababa the Ethiopian government set a limit to the quotas of accommodation and cars provided and delegates in excess of the fixed quotas thus became the responsibility of their own governments. It was also necessary to provide competent secretarial and administrative services for the delegation.

On the eve of the Conference the Publicity Secretariat made arrangements for Kojo Botsio to launch Nkrumah's *Africa Must Unite* in Addis Ababa. That Secretariat worked in close liaison with Sam Morris who relayed daily reports on the Conference proceedings to Radio Ghana while the Ghana News Agency representative maintained contact with Reuters. Every Ghanaian delegate (and there were some 100 Ministers, politicians, civil servants, ambassadors, 'activists', military and security personnel) was thoroughly briefed for the meeting, and some were sent several days ahead of the main body in order to lobby other conference members on Ghana's position. When the Conference assembled Nkrumah spoke passionately in support of his views on continental unity. It was a long speech, following very closely the ideas he had put forward in his message to the heads of state and in *Africa Must Unite*.

Other heads of state were in no mood to adopt any radical changes in sovereignty which might in their view alter the *status quo* in Africa. For them, nothing more was necessary than a loose organization which catered for certain specific services. Neither reason nor emotion could persuade them as a group to change that view.* Instead of an executive

---

* Many of the States did not possess the economic independence that would have enabled them to seek the kind of 'pooling' of resources that Nkrumah's proposals envisaged. As late as 1971 *West Africa* noted that France had set aside cash 'to wipe out possible Dahomeyan budget deficits' (31 December 1971).

panel and a chairman, who would be responsible for dealing with all-African problems, the Conference decided to establish a 'Secretariat' run by a non-political administrative Secretary-General; instead of the call for a high command and a parliament, the African leaders agreed only to a defence commission and a council of ministers with no legislative powers. It seemed that Nkrumah had blown the trumpet of unity too loud and long, thereby deafening the other heads of state. They were not prepared to give way to his ideas. It would however be naive to conclude that failure to attain African unity was a result of President Nkrumah's trumpeting too loudly about it. The real issue seems to be that his expectations were not based on an accurate analysis of the forces behind the heads of state which made it impossible for them to go further with him on the question of a continental government for Africa.

Even the naming of the organization set up by the Conference proved very difficult. In the end Nkrumah succeeded in the nick of time in getting President Maga to provide the title 'Organisation of African Unity'. He was obviously extremely satisfied at this last-minute retrieval of the concept of unity from the rubble-heap of his disappointment. President Maga's memory had served him well. A few days before the Conference he and Nkrumah had had a secret all-night meeting at a Ghanaian training college in Pusiga on the northernmost outpost of Ghana's border with Togo in order to discuss the full details of Nkrumah's proposals.

DIPLOMACY BY CONFERENCE

Nkrumah made considerable use of conferences in the promotion of the African image. During the period under review, the highlights were those in Accra in April 1958, in Casablanca in 1961, in Addis Ababa in 1963, and finally in Accra in 1965. For each of these meetings he set the target of drawing the African states closer to his ideal of unity. From each he tried to salvage some concrete gain, as a mark of progress, even when he failed to achieve his immediate and direct objective.

The 1958 Conference lessened the significance of the Sahara as a barrier between Arab and Black Africa. It also agreed that the independent African states should set up a permanent mission for joint consultation at the United Nations. The 1961 Casablanca Conference set up a joint 'African' High Command with headquarters in Accra.

Also from the same source one finds a report that the 'French Air Force has been authorized to purchase a DC-8 for its operations in Chad'. The conditions that make such involvement of external powers possible are not conducive to unity on a continental basis.

Addis Ababa in 1963 provided a climax. In terms of concrete achievements, the 1965 Conference in Accra was a disappointment.* Nkrumah introduced a new concept of intra-African relationships by stimulating and encouraging a kind of diplomacy by conference. He supported or initiated regular all-African meetings on labour, sports, exchange of information by radio and the press, etc.

The administrative arrangements at Ghana's official conferences were always thorough and comprehensive. Nothing was left to chance, for Nkrumah insisted on approving personally every detail of the preparations. Delegates were nominated on the basis of their acquaintance with the subjects to be considered. For this purpose, officials normally put forward the names of those whom they considered to have the kind of expertise demanded. They also took into account whatever information they had at their disposal about the strength (numerical and qualitative) of other delegations. Such information was often received through coded messages from our diplomatic representatives abroad. In certain cases it was possible to secure particulars of the positions which opposing delegations were expected to take.

Procedure for the nomination and ultimate appointment of delegates may be summarized as follows:

(i) appropriate divisions of the Ministry or Secretariat nominated candidates—Ministers, Members of Parliament, party representatives, university lecturers, or other public officers—giving brief notes on the experience of each candidate and indicating why the nomination had been made;

* Much was made at the time of the fact of Ghana's 'subversion' of neighbouring states such as the Ivory Coast, Nigeria, etc. because of the presence in Ghana of elements from those states who were opposed to the policies of their governments. This subject has been discussed elsewhere in this study. In retrospect one can see that the real conflict was not that of personalities at all. The 1965 Conference failed to achieve the high hopes that Nkrumah had entertained for it because (a) the heads of state were not ready to divest themselves of their extra-African entanglements to enter a purely African organization; (b) Nkrumah had not then succeeded in building broad-based support across the continent for his continental structure. Without this there was no foundation for the superstructure of continental government. (It is significant, in this connection, to note that the articles of the OAU Charter began with the words 'We, Heads of State . . .' Where were their people?); (c) Nkrumah's dedication to unity was so intense and his hurry and haste for it so furious that on occasion it led him to overlook some of the objective realities. It should also be noted that within Ghana itself support for continental unity had waned, except within the ranks of a small body of party zealots and activists. These elements did not appear to be fully seized with the complexities of the problems which continental government involved. To many of them its realization depended primarily on the vehemence with which the cause could be advocated. They more or less believed that it really was just round the corner.

(ii) these were submitted through the official Head of the Ministry or Secretariat (who sometimes altered or amended them) to the Minister;

(iii) the Minister then amended, if necessary, before putting the list to the President;

(iv) usually the list was returned to the Minister with full notes of Nkrumah's reactions to the proposals. Sometimes names were eliminated or added. The reasons for any change were not always given, although one often saw remarks such as 'X is unsuitable, I have suggested Y' or 'not ideologically sound, *speak*'. In the latter case the Minister would approach the President before approval could be given. The Minister and the President usually appointed the leader of each delegation. If a delegation did not include a Minister, it was headed by Ghana's Ambassador whenever meetings were held in a country where there was a Mission. In that event, he received his briefing by coded message or by letter through the delegation.

(v) the list was returned to the Permanent Secretary (Official Head) for follow-up action, such as notification of delegates, briefing, transport arrangements, provision of expenses, communications, and the selection of supporting officials to provide conference and secretarial services. Those duties were accordingly 'farmed out' to the various divisions of the Ministry or Secretariat. Briefing was usually undertaken by official letter signed by the Permanent Secretary/Minister, if delegates were of the rank of MP or above. Delegations composed of Ministers and Members of Parliament were invariably briefed by the Minister himself, unless he had previously delegated this task to the official Head of the Office. Briefing consisted of an outline or summary of the field of interest of the conference; its historical, economic, and political implications; reasons for Ghana's interest; the standpoint Ghana wished to take, and why; if voting was involved at the Conference, the nature of Ghana's vote, and delegations that could be supported by Ghana in the voting, together with the reasons for this; what kind of lobbying might be undertaken before and during the Conference, and which members of the delegation might initiate such lobbying.

At the end of each Conference two reports were usually provided:

(a) *a verbal report* on salient points, including impressions of personalities at the Conference and indications as to what future course Ghana might follow. This report was made direct to the President with the Minister (and sometimes the Official Head) in attendance. Nkrumah was particularly keen on this ritual and was known to set aside whatever business he had in hand for it, sometimes waiting up all night for delegations, in order to receive this kind of report.

(b) *a fully documented report* giving details of the course of the Conference and conclusions reached. This was usually submitted to the Official Head of the Ministry/Secretariat who then prepared it in the form of a memo, either for the Cabinet or for the Minister or President. Decisions reached on the report had to be duly circulated for public information at home—in the form of a press release—and for the guidance of Ghana's overseas missions. Consequential action, if any, was prepared by the Ministry/Secretariat. If such action involved expenditure of funds for which no provision existed in the Estimates, a fresh memo was submitted either to the Minister or President or to the Cabinet for approval to incur such expenditure. A specimen minute is given in Appendix C.

5

POLICY PRACTICE OUTSIDE AFRICA

After Nkrumah's visit to Eastern Europe in 1961, his decision to set up Ghanaian embassies in every state of the Eastern bloc, though economically indefensible, had the immediate political effect of extending the limits of knowledge about Ghana abroad. By such a seemingly rash approach and through the clever use of propaganda—in the best sense of the term—Nkrumah succeeded in creating a world audience for his policy statements. His propaganda involved much detailed paperwork and the preparation of memoranda based on extensive research. He had a passion for facts and figures and left nothing to chance in so far as the written word was concerned. To this end he maintained a private team of research experts, studying current world affairs, running a news clipping service, and building up a systematic record and analysis of events.

Most of the decisions he took involving foreign governments were subject to previous scrutiny for legal propriety by the Attorney-General, who was a constant consultant and adviser. This gave Geoffrey Bing, who was in that post for a long period, considerable influence with the President in both internal and external policy-making. His expert knowledge of the law in its many ramifications was most useful to Nkrumah.

It cannot be denied that during Nkrumah's regime Ghana's pan-African posture put her in the forefront of African affairs. It helped to raise the black man in the eyes of the world; Africa took on a new image and prominence, usually described by Nkrumah in terms of the 'African personality'.[32] By 1960, inspired by the example of Ghana's independence, a large number of other African states welcomed the opportunity of participating in international negotiation.

The first team of Ghanaian diplomats appointed to missions outside Africa were men who would have done great credit to any country, such as Sir Edward Asafu-Adjaye and Daniel Chapman, Ghana's representatives in London and Washington respectively. It was recognized, however, that in the pursuit of external relations it was not enough to have capable men. There was also the importance of maintaining well defined areas of policy.

THE UNITED NATIONS

In the practice of Ghana's external relations three areas of policy may be identified. These were the establishment of the 'African presence', decolonization through the United Nations, and non-alignment. The aspects of Ghana's policy contributing to the creation of the African presence has already been discussed. This chapter deals primarily with the UN and non-alignment.

Admission to the 13th Session of the United Nations General Assembly as a sovereign independent state in September 1957 gave Ghana an opportunity to work with like-minded states for the decolonization of the African continent. Ghana was free to link up with the independent states noted for their anti-colonial policies, such as the United States, Canada, India, and the Eastern European countries. This necessitated the observance of the policy of non-alignment.

Ghana's United Nations office was staffed by a specially selected team whose duties included the preparation of draft documents for the Head of Mission, service on UN Committees, and organized 'lobbying'. It was also required to assist delegations attending UN meetings from Ghana with the preparation of official reports. The Ghana UN mission had special responsibility to maintain close links with the African UN group established as a result of the first Conference of Independent African States. The mission provided a secretary for that group. By this means Ghana sought to harmonize its anti-colonial policies with those of other African states.

Particularly close links existed between the UN mission and the Ministry in Accra. Whenever there were important issues before the General Assembly, such as the Congo crisis or Rhodesia's threat to declare unilateral independence, Nkrumah held frequent meetings with his political and official advisers. These included Gbedemah, Botsio, Kofi Baako, Tawia Adamafio, and John Tettegah. The composition of the body of advisers changed according to the nature of the subject discussed, or to the shift of power within the CPP. Kweku Boateng, Tawia Adamafio, and Kwasi Amoako-Atta gained considerable prominence politically.

Before any subject was discussed, officials were required to circulate a paper; decisions taken after such discussions were embodied in a note submitted to the President or the Foreign Minister for approval in the form of instructions to the UN representative. Such messages were often transmitted by telex in code or *en clair*, the particular medium of communication employed being determined by the delicacy of the subject. On voting procedures the Ghana representative at the UN was allowed considerable discretion within the framework of policy.

On the two occasions (1960, 1961) that Nkrumah addressed the United Nations General Assembly, the Cabinet Office, the Ministry of Foreign Affairs, and Ghana's Permanent Mission at the UN were entrusted with responsibility for the arrangements. On the 1961 visit Nkrumah was received by President Kennedy at the White House. Preparation for the visit included the composition of the President's delegation and the provision of suitable accommodation in New York for the President and the other members of the delegation, which included Ako Adjei, Foreign Minister, Krobo Edusei, Minister of Interior, Kweku Boateng, Minister of Information, and Tawia Adamafio, officials, security and publicity staffs. Geoffrey Bing, Attorney-General, also attended as Legal Adviser. Enoch Okoh, Secretary to the Cabinet, and I set up an office in the President's hotel and established a working party for drafting purposes, consisting of the Minister of Foreign Affairs, the Attorney-General, Ghana's UN Representative, the Cabinet Secretary, and the Permanent Secretary for Foreign Affairs. A preliminary draft speech for the President had been produced by the Ministry before the delegation's departure. Nevertheless this was revised in the light of discussion with Alex Quaison-Sackey, then Ghana's UN representative. The final draft produced by the working party was submitted to the President, who revised it, as always, in line with his peculiar form and style.

Ghana's role in the United Nations depended very much on the degree of coordination that could be achieved between Accra and Ghana's delegation in New York. The swiftness with which the pace of world events moved, and the relatively limited resources of the Ministry, meant that there were often gaps which led to complaints from the Ghana Mission about inadequate briefing or failure to convey up-to-date reports about developments in policy. By 1964 Ghana's prestige and influence at the UN had nevertheless risen to such a pitch that her representative, Alex Quaison-Sackey, was elected President of the General Assembly.

NON-ALIGNMENT

Supporting anti-colonialism and at the same time maintaining good relations with the Western powers was a very difficult political game. This was obvious in the third area of Ghana's external policy—non-alignment. By historical tradition Ghana's political future was bound up with that of Britain, with which she shared the Commonwealth fellowship. It would have been unwise for Ghana to turn her back on Britain. Ghana was more impressed by the example of India than that of Burma, which had chosen to leave the Commonwealth after gaining independence. Ghana's ethnic ties with neighbouring French-speaking states made close relations with France practically indispensable. Owing to the Sahara atom tests and the French government's paternalism towards her former colonies, however, the development of such relations under the Nkrumah regime proved difficult. In so far as the United States was concerned, her strong support at the United Nations for the process of decolonization in Africa and her position as the greatest economic force in the post-war world made the forging of close links between her and Ghana an imperative necessity.

Ghana's decision to draw closer to Eastern Europe was a means of expressing in concrete terms her freedom of action. Ghana found herself standing between the two world giants, compelled by her need to draw on both for technical and material aid.

Nkrumah showed great interest in Commonwealth meetings, which he usually attended in person. The delegation often included the Foreign Minister and the Ministers of Justice and Finance, together with officials of the Cabinet Office, Ministry of Foreign Affairs, Ministry of Finance or Trade, and the Department of Statistics. The most senior officials accompanied him to the conference room, two at a time, working in shifts. His interventions were always vigorous, and calculated to elicit support for the African cause within the Commonwealth. Perhaps his most significant contribution to the Commonwealth connection was his proposal at the 1964 Conference for the establishment of a Commonwealth Secretariat. In the last year of his regime Ghana broke off relations with Britain to support the 1965 OAU resolution over Rhodesia's unilateral declaration of independence.

In August and September 1961 Nkrumah toured Europe and attended the Belgrade Conference of the non-aligned powers in order to emphasize his commitment. No official visit was made to the East German Democratic Republic, as the West German representative in Ghana had made it clear that this would be regarded by his government as a hostile act. As the government of Ghana was hoping at that time to obtain a £2,000,000 loan from West Germany for a second bridge over the Volta, in order to provide a direct fast route to Togo, Nkrumah bowed to their wishes. This understanding did not, however, prevent Nkrumah from making a brief stop-over in East Berlin while on a visit to Prague. At the Humboldt University he was awarded an honorary doctorate in economic sciences. Among those present at the ceremony were the Vice-Chairman of the State Council of the German Democratic Republic and the Deputy Premier.

THE ABORTIVE HANOI TRIP

The war in Vietnam had been discussed at the Commonwealth Prime Ministers' Conference in June 1965. At that meeting the Prime Ministers had expressed their intention of 'sending a mission of their own', comprising the heads of government of the United Kingdom, Ghana, Nigeria, and Trinidad and Tobago to explore peace-making possibilities, to the capitals mainly concerned with the conflict, but this proposal came to nothing. In early June a British junior Minister, Harold Davies, paid a five-day visit to Hanoi. In December the Pope made special appeals for the restoration of peace. In spite of the failure of the Commonwealth peace mission, President Nkrumah had reason to believe that the prospect of peace in Vietnam was not altogether bleak. It would certainly be a great credit to Africa, and the developing world in general, if the initiative for peace in Vietnam could come from that source. Nkrumah's concern for Vietnam was greatly stimulated by a personal invitation to visit Hanoi, which he received in July 1965 from President Ho Chi Minh. He sent Kwesi Armah, then Ghana High Commissioner in London, with a delegation to meet the Hanoi authorities on the spot, and to work out details of a programme for the visit. After many difficulties *en route*, particularly in Moscow, where Kwesi Armah's delegation was told there was no room on the Soviet plane travelling through Irkutsk, the Ghanaians reached Hanoi. Here the delegation was told by Ho Chi Minh that he would be pleased to see Nkrumah but that he doubted whether a peace mission would serve a useful purpose at the time, as the Vietnamese were hoping to score a major victory over the Americans with the onset of the monsoon.

Meanwhile, Alex Quaison-Sackey, newly appointed Foreign Minister after his service as President of the United Nations General Assembly, was sent to Washington with a special message from Nkrumah to President Johnson. It was brief, informing the American President of Hanoi's invitation and appealing to him for the suspension of American bombing in Hanoi during Nkrumah's visit. If this suspension had been achieved, it would have been a happy prelude to the effort Nkrumah was making towards the cessation of hostilities. Johnson's reply was terse and lacking in enthusiasm but it contained a memorable, and what officials like myself in Flagstaff House considered to be an ominous, passage: 'If you go to Hanoi, Mr President, you will be in no danger of American military action in Vietnam.' Moreover, this reply was delivered to Nkrumah, not by the US Ambassador, Franklyn Williams, but by his Counsellor, Mr Foley. Franklyn Williams himself was at that time absent from Accra 'on trek' in Ashanti. When he became US

Ambassador in Ghana, he had attempted to get close to Nkrumah, inviting him to collaborate in setting up a Lincolnian Old Boys' Society in Ghana. Nkrumah evinced no interest, suspecting him of CIA links. Andrew Tully's book on the CIA, copies of which Alex Quaison-Sackey had sent to Nkrumah, probably did more damage to Ghana–US relations than any other written work.

Officials instructed to make arrangements for the visit to Hanoi, Enoch Okoh, Fred Arkhurst, and myself, were beginning to read much between the lines, and were unhappy about the whole proposal. We lost no time in expressing our forebodings;* but in spite of this the Ministry of Foreign Affairs was instructed to prepare a suitable brief on the Vietnam issue for the President. When this brief was delivered, Okoh decided to summarize it in a form which could easily be grasped by the President within the time available.

Every effort made by various associates and friends of the President to dissuade him from making the journey proved unavailing. It had been made clear that British initiatives and the Pope's appeals for peace had produced few positive results. Nkrumah seemed to feel, however, that if he failed to honour Ho Chi Minh's invitation he would let down an Asian leader for whom he had the greatest respect. He thought that the delicate prospect of peace in Vietnam could hang on the thin thread of his proposed visit. He also indicated that if he did not go to Vietnam he would seem to be lacking in courage and resolution, trying to preserve his own life when thousands of Americans and Indo-Chinese were dying on the battlefields and in the towns every day. The consequence of that unfinished journey is now history.

* Everyone had an eerie sense of things not somehow being right, and I was personally unhappy about something 'in the air' without being able to identify it specifically. I also did not think that it was in keeping with the normal sense of diplomatic propriety that an important message from President Johnson should have been delivered to President Nkrumah by a Counsellor at the US embassy, and not by the Ambassador himself. Throughout the course of the journey to Hanoi I was aware of secret doubts about the mission which made me vaguely apprehensive of its results. For example, at Cairo Airport the banners of welcome were expressed in such terms as 'Long Live Ghana/Long Live President Nasser'. Why, for the first time in my experience, was Nasser being juxtaposed with Ghana and not with Nkrumah? I called Enoch Okoh's attention to this strange and un-Egyptian form of protocol but said nothing more about it. My mind was too occupied with intuitive and vague imaginings to work on anything positive.

6

AFRICAN ADMINISTRATION

In this the final chapter it is necessary to summarize my impressions of how Nkrumah saw the machinery which he inherited from colonial rule and the use to which he tried to put it.

In the first place, it should be stated that from the very eve of independence Nkrumah had no illusions as to the nature of the opposition that he would face.[33] He had to deal with a traditionally oriented community in which power had resided in a chiefly order that had been brought to heel by colonial rule and made to serve its imperial ends. The British administration had faced the opposition of an elitist group which had managed to rely on the clandestine, covert, and muffled support of that chiefly order in return for assurances of some measure of traditional power on independence. Nkrumah, on the other hand, impatient of chiefly rule, had seen it as an obstacle to progress, as an unnecessary hurdle in the march of the 'common man' towards the establishment of a new egalitarianism which would remove all privilege resulting from 'position' and 'station in life'. It was in this spirit that he demanded cooperation and association with the new order, in place of the dying age of the colonial regime. He even went on to warn that if they failed to react in this way the chiefs would 'run away and leave their sandals behind'. He had removed the colonial power but he was also building up in its place a formidable internal opposition to his regime. If the colonial regime had transferred political power to the traditional order (as indeed had seemed the case, right up to the time of the CPP's victory in the first national elections in 1951), there would have been the interesting irony of Britain with its concept of Westminster rule transferring power to a traditional elite.

The whole question of whether the government of the future independent nation of Ghana would assume the character of administration based on foreign models or whether it would operate on the model of traditional ideas of government was one of the fundamental causes of difference between the chiefs, the late Kobina Sekyi, and Nkrumah. Sekyi had written an article in 1950 entitled 'The Best Constitutions Are Born, Not Made', warning Ghanaians on the eve of the establishment of ministerial government that the mere adoption of a western style constitution was no guarantee of freedom or stability. In his view, based probably on his long association with the African traditional polity through the Aborigines' Rights Protection Society, only an administration which was founded on the organs of government evolved by Africans could secure permanent acceptance by the people and ultimate growth. Perhaps not in Ghana only, but in all the developing nations of Africa, further examination of lawyer Sekyi's warning on the use of western-style constitutions to the abandonment of the original concepts of government in Africa would prove beneficial.

On the other hand, Nkrumah seemed concerned about the fact that the British would never hand over power to the people unless the administration they were called upon to surrender was cast in a constitutional mould which their parliament and people could understand and recognize.[34] It was from this standpoint that he distrusted both the traditional order and the colonial administration which he took over. As he stated quite clearly in his autobiography, the colonial concept of a civil service was a misnomer 'because the civil servants were in effect civil masters'. Nkrumah's main preoccupation in so far as the civil service was concerned was to rid it of all its 'governing' proclivities and to reduce it to its proper level as the instrument of government, its executive arm. This, in part, accounts for the difficulties expressed earlier in this study about having career diplomats appointed as ambassadors because the position of ambassador carried not only the element of diplomatic prestige but was also seen as an instrument of authority at the policy-making level. It also accounts for the fact that a new civil service code enacted by an act of legislation after the change of constitution in 1960 removed some of the civil service orders entrenched in the 1957 independence constitution. Bing has pointed out that the entrenchment of civil service codes within the constitution was meant by the British government to 'provide for government by Civil Servants behind a Parliamentary façade'.[35]

Nkrumah's conception of the civil service was clear and, on the basis of the colonial experience, rather radical. He demanded not only direct participation of the civil service in the execution of the government's policies but also full identification with its aspirations, agreeing with Nyerere that 'Top civil servants gifted with administrative skills and imbued with the fervour of independence and the hope of development are vital to the reconstruction of a State; for even the best plans will go awry if they are not handled with heart as well as head'.[36]

Between Nkrumah and the colonial government there was a serious difference over the role of the civil service. To the colonial order the importance of the civil service administration meant that it had to be separated from the political order; for Nkrumah that importance was the very reason why the government should have control over it. I have pointed out elsewhere in this study that the colonial view is neither observed nor supported in practice in any metropolitan state. As indicated earlier, Nkrumah saw the concept of a non-political civil service as colonialism's strategy for 'using indigenous administrators to run a regime that serves the interests of a foreign power'. In view of the quotation from Dr Fleming cited in Chapter 1 Nkrumah's accusation should be seen as reflecting his basic suspicion of the civil service machinery even when it was manned by his own people. As one who was brought up in the colonial service, I know that that suspicion was unfounded. When the civil servants opposed any scheme of government, it was either because they did not share the politician's optimism about its success or because there were no adequate funds to carry it out. In my long experience of service with African colleagues, I cannot say that anyone deliberately sought to run down any national project which was properly conceived.

The role of the bureaucrats in the course of these developments deserves some attention. Under the Nkrumah regime the administration was run along two parallel lines—the processes of the party functionaries or politicians, and those of the civil service. In the Foreign Service the trained civil servants were at home with work carried out on the lines of what has been described as 'orthodox diplomacy', using the methods acquired during training under the British.

Under the colonial administration the civil servant had legislative and administrative functions which were clearly of a political nature. No public servant could therefore be expected to escape involvement in the political implications of his official actions. But Nkrumah was not a keen supporter of the methods of administration inherited from the British. To him the routine procedures of administrative coordination were all in the nature of 'red tape' bureaucracy, which he considered both time-consuming and frustrating. After 1960, with the republican constitution and the passing of a new Civil Service Act, the head of state also became head of the civil service. He was thus in a position to control appointments and promotions within it. The civil service was in this manner almost completely absorbed into the political system.

This is the period in which the Secretariat form of administration was instituted. Lionel Tiger[37] gives the impression that Nkrumah was familiar with the USA and White House administration, and that he had been influenced by Kennedy's type of presidential administration. While this may have been a contributing factor, it should be mentioned that 1961 was a particularly difficult year for the regime: the year of the *Dawn Broadcast*, the second Sekondi-Takoradi strike, the removal from office of some of Nkrumah's old associates, internal suspicions among party bosses—all these created a situation where Nkrumah showed a marked lack of confidence in certain Ministers and ministerial government generally, thus encouraging him to rely more and more on civil servants, who were placed in direct charge of the Secretariats under his personal surveillance and control.

For the diplomats change of authority did not imply change of methods of work. They continued to study problems raised by the policies of the government, analysed the facts, and carefully weighed all sides of every question at issue. The results of such consideration were then put up to their Ministers, Ambassadors, etc., who then made their decisions in the light of prevailing political circumstances. Sometimes the diplomats would be invited to a discussion before a decision was made. This afforded a further opportunity to press home any particular points deserving special attention. Every government expects the best work of its civil servants; on this there could be no difference of opinion; and, as a general rule, the weaker a government is, the more likely it is to rely on its trained personnel.

THE AFRICAN WAY

It is important to draw a line between the African way of doing things—if this can be clearly defined—and the beaten track of formal administrative practice. What is really meant by 'the African way'? Africa has such diversity of customs, cultures, attitudes, stages of development, that it would be misleading to base absolute judgements on any issues about that 'way'. In the field of administration traditional African society did not have a 'science' as one understands the term today. The term 'African way' is, therefore, applied loosely to indicate an attitude of mind rather than a formal system. Furthermore, whenever it becomes necessary for any reason to discard routine administration, the African way should be employed without reserve by both parties concerned with its application. When one side plays the African game and the other does not it often leads to serious embarrassment and sometimes even to disastrous results. In those circumstances, any resort to more orthodox administrative practices becomes almost futile, degenerating into a clumsy and ineffective improvisation.

The case of Kulungugu illustrates this point. In August 1962 a miniature summit meeting had been arranged between Nkrumah and President Yameogo of Upper Volta. The meeting was to take place at a little-known frontier outpost named Tenkudugu, a few miles from Bawku on the northern boundary between Togo, Ghana, and Upper Volta. The two heads of state had agreed to discuss outstanding financial and economic problems and the means by which trade between the two countries—agreed upon under the 'Paga' frontier arrangements—could be more firmly consolidated. In July 1961 Ghana and Upper Volta had concluded a commercial agreement. On 16 June 1961 there was the ceremony of 'breaking the barrier' at Paga, a frontier post between Ghana and Upper Volta. The ceremony consisted of knocking down a symbolic wall between the two countries. It was performed by Yameogo and Nkrumah. A joint Ghana-Upper Volta Commission was set up to study the economic implications of the new agreement. As a result of this study, Ghana gave Upper Volta £2,000,000* which represented the equivalent of the Ghana customs surcharge on Upper Volta goods transported through Ghana.

At the official level elaborate preparations had been made including the exchange of 'position' papers on the subjects for discussion, together with approved lists of delegations on both sides. Whenever Nkrumah was on tour in Ghana, it was the practice to have in addition to his approved party (ministers, civil servants and party officials, security and intelligence staffs, press representatives and photographers), a large concourse of nondescript 'camp-followers' who often travelled at their own expense. On this visit the practice was faithfully observed. There were large numbers of party representatives, market-women, and all sorts of unclassifiable followers. The party had stopped in Tamale for the night, and was due to continue the journey through the Upper Region of Ghana to Tenkudugu the next day. The last stop on the route was at the rather large and rambling northern outpost of Bawku. Before the party set out to enter Voltaic territory, I called the two senior Ministers, Adamafio and Ako Adjei, and pointed out to them that it would be embarrassing for the President to attend the meeting with such a large crowd who were not on the delegation and had no specific responsibilities in the discussions. I stated that the official

---

* My attention has been drawn to the details concerning the granting of the loan of £2,000,000 to Upper Volta. The specific circumstances were as follows: 'The funds which Ghana gave Upper Volta were an advance in respect of customs duties collected in Ghanaian ports on goods destined for Upper Volta. It was agreed that Upper Volta should import goods through Ghana without paying customs duties. To implement this decision, duties would be levied on goods at Ghanaian ports whether destined for Upper Volta or not. But records would be kept of goods leaving Ghana for Upper Volta. From the records the customs duties which had been paid would be calculated and refunded to Upper Volta. But Upper Volta wanted some money immediately and two million pounds sterling was advanced against the refunds promised' (K. B. Asante). At the time when this agreement was concluded with Upper Volta, the Voltaics were seeking the use of alternative port facilities to their traditional use of Abidjan harbour in the Ivory Coast, owing to current strain between Presidents Houphouet-Boigny and Yameogo. The strain did not apparently last long enough to make continued need for port facilities in Ghana imperative.

delegation, including the President's personal staff, did not exceed thirty persons. What would the Voltaic government do to provide additional accommodation and food if we literally 'dumped' so many Ghanaians on them without previous warning? I needed authority to explain the circumstances of their journey to the unauthorized followers, and to send everyone who was not on the delegation back home. One Minister muttered something about not worrying, and being over-meticulous. In desperation, and anxious to avoid both disgrace for Ghana and embarrassment for the Voltaics, I asked that we should put the matter to the President himself. Enoch Okoh, the Cabinet Secretary, supported me at this stage. Nkrumah, noting that Adamafio and Ako Adjei were not sure about the wisdom of turning so many followers back, just shrugged us off with the response that our objections were irrelevant—we were all Africans going to brother Africans, and had no need to be finicky about hospitality. The result was that the Ghanaians virtually made a 'triumphal entry' into Tenkudugu. Considering the modest size of the village, it was like wielding a sledge-hammer to swat a fly. But our fears about accommodation and feeding were justified. Ministers were forced to sleep three to a bed. The food, although adequate for the approved delegation, was not sufficient for the large number of additional followers. It was in these circumstances that Tawia Adamafio, Ako Adjei, and H. H. Cofie-Crabbe had to share one room for the night (31 July 1962). The next day, 1 August, on the return journey, another 'African act' took place. The President's party was asked to stop at a point unscheduled in the programme. Within minutes of his alighting from the car to receive a bouquet from a young schoolboy, representing a small 'bush school' by the road-side, a hand grenade was thrown at him. The explosion narrowly missed him, although some pellets found their way into his back, but the innocent boy received a direct hit and was killed.

This account has been given to emphasize two points. First, Tawia Adamafio, Ako Adjei, and H. H. Cofie-Crabbe were subsequently charged with complicity in the assassination plot. The fact that on the night of the 31 July the three of them shared a room in Tenkudugu appeared to have given weight to suspicions about their complicity. If official advice about travelling to Upper Volta on the basis of approved arrangements had been observed, at least that piece of evidence could not have been brought against them. Second, the unscheduled stop had been made in order to satisfy the chance request of a Ghanaian not concerned with the arrangements for the journey. If the request had been turned down when it was made to the President, whoever made that attempt on his life would have had to seek another opportunity. It is also of interest to record that when the incident occurred it was the 'administration' which quickly stepped in the breach to organize positive measures for dealing with the situation. We sent K. B. Asante ahead to alert the medical centre at Bawku to be ready to deal with the urgent casualty cases; he was also to use the facilities of the police signals at Bawku to send confidential reports of the assassination attempt to the regional headquarters in Tamale and the central administration in Accra.

Another effect of Kulungugu may be mentioned here. It marked a new low in the morale and effectiveness of the CPP. Earlier in this study the influence of the new group of young party stalwarts, which had succeeded in supplanting the power of the old party bosses who were supposed to have lost their socialist fervour, was noted. That activist vanguard, with its often clamant ideological vigour, seemed to have gained strength under Adamafio's energetic leadership. Adamafio's capacity for work was enormous. He was outstanding by rigorous civil service standards as a prolific and efficient draftsman. These qualities endeared him to Nkrumah. When Adamafio lost favour, having been linked by the Intelligence Organization with the assassination attempt, a decisive blow was dealt to the prestige and influence of the activist vanguard. Nkrumah was thus left between two stools. Having virtually abandoned his old associates he was now to lose the energetic intervention of the party activists. This led to his heavy reliance on the civil service and the military for the maintenance of his administration and to a period of political isolation. The CPP, as a political organ, had apparently suffered the blow which all revolutionary parties eventually suffer. Having been installed in power by massive nationalist fervour which became an effective weapon for the overthrow of colonial rule, they lost, or ceased to bring into full play, the secret of political consensus with which they established that power, and disintegration became inevitable.

It is easy to confuse the 'African way' with proper and correct procedures for action. Until African bureaucrats have evolved recognized 'African' procedures of administration, they must be on their guard for possible conflicts between the African style and certain forms of recognized protocol.

An 'African' style of administration would be difficult to define, just as one cannot identify an African capitalist or engineer. The practices that concern the development of recognized habits and activities that are human cannot be classified racially. It must be accepted, however, that certain universal habits are performed differently in different parts of the world, and even in different areas in the same country, owing to marked differences in environmental situations. Thus the civil engineer using the same basic engineering methods in Africa may construct a given bridge in a manner perhaps different from the system he would adopt were he to build a similar bridge in the Arctic Circle. For practically identical reasons the African civil servant needs to examine his administrative problems in the light of the human 'climate' in which he operates. For example, in a country like Africa, where every effort is needed to obtain rapid all-round development, administrative cadres cannot talk realistically of a four-day work-week, as an affluent society such as the United States can afford to do. Similarly, a Foreign Service official in another African state would be more identified with the legitimate aspirations of that African state than with those of a non-African government operating in the same area.

It must be emphasized that it is in the recognition of the importance of observing certain fundamental values such as honesty, integrity, punctuality, concern for the under-privileged, and devotion to duty that one must seek the expression of an African style of doing things in administration. Nearly all these virtues were the original values respected in African societies in which the individualist view of existence was always deprecated. In times when the need for total rehabilitation of the African life and image is as paramount as in the period of change from colonial to independent status, does the African require to be reminded of that past?

The 1966 February coup brought to an end one form and style of administration but one vital lesson which I hope this study reveals is the need to avoid importing administrative models from outside Africa. The continent had no identifiable system or practice of administration which could be used under modern conditions. The indigenous administrator in Ghana, as indeed in all Africa, has a responsibility to re-examine his methods and processes of work, in the peculiar circumstances in which he has to perform his duties. His task is to seek to secure a synthesis of the best elements from his own past and the new ideas which his contacts with a changing world bring to his notice.

I must confess that, as a trained official, I was often nettled and exasperated by President Nkrumah's unorthodox methods, his unconcealed distaste for the slow pace of bureaucracy. He, and other leaders like him in Africa, regarded that pace, that necessary reliance upon system and analysis, which appeared to be excessively time-consuming, as a deliberate attempt to sabotage the efforts of politicians. This is unfortunate, because officials are no less patriotic than politicians. Indeed, this sense of patriotism, this Africanness in me, and my own anxiety about the relatively slow rate of progress in Africa, sometimes evoked my sympathy for the politicians' desire to break through routine procedures—'damn the consequences', as they often said impatiently. Besides, one cannot ignore the fact that neither the orthodox nor the unorthodox method is without weaknesses and shortcomings. Sometimes a refusal to wait for the processes and procedures to be followed arises from a genuine concern for haste. It can however be used to cover up abuse of public office and to conceal corrupt practices. If attempts are made to cut through so-called red tape, it is of paramount importance that together with those attempts African states should develop new guidelines to prevent corruption, nepotism, and misuse of influence. Such a development must be closely linked with the political institutions being established in the African states and the extent to which they are adapted to the needs of the people as a whole and not to just a part of the citizenry. It must therefore be obvious that the official would be following a disastrous course if he condemned either method outright before he had time to examine both carefully and dispassionately. The Ghana Foreign Service, which is its country's 'window on the world', is particularly well placed to make this kind of positive and constructive contribution to administrative practice in Ghana. Serving Africa in that spirit is a legitimate aspiration.

APPENDIX A

Having secured Ghana's independence, Nkrumah lost no time in rally-
ing support in Africa for the pan-African cause. To this end he summoned the first Conference of independent African states in Accra
which took place from 15 to 22 April 1958. All the eight independent
African states attended. Only South Africa was absent although she
had been invited. As she had made her acceptance conditional upon
invitations also being sent to the colonial powers, she virtually excluded
herself. The fact that the states of North Africa had agreed to cross the
Sahara to attend the conference was in itself the first positive sign of
success for the Conference. The coming together of the northern and
western states of Africa removed the symbol of separation between the
two areas once and for all—the Sahara no longer divided north from
southern Africa.

In making arrangements for this Conference the Foreign Service
was faced with its first major challenge. There was, for example, the
preparation of the agenda and other papers, such as notes on the subjects
that might be considered by the delegates. There were protocol
problems, such as the correct form of address of each leader of the
delegations, or of precedence for the seating of delegates on formal
occasions, the provision of liaison officers for delegations, distribution
of cars, allocation of accommodation, and so on. The agenda for the
Conference included foreign policy questions, the future of independent
territories in Africa, maintenance and protection of the sovereignty of
the African states, promotion of economic cooperation among them,
based on exchange of technical, scientific, and educational information,
and problems of international peace. Arrangements were also made for
each delegation to be met on arrival, with a guard of honour, salute,
and its national anthem. It is to the credit of the Foreign Office and its
official head, A. L. Adu, that these responsibilities were borne satisfac-
torily and without serious administrative mishap.

Only two minor lapses occurred but these were rapidly disposed of.
The first was the demand by the Arabic-speaking North African states
that Arabic should be one of the official languages (the others being
English and French). The Arab delegates indicated that for this purpose

they were prepared to provide bilingual interpreters. The Conference however appealed to their Arabic-speaking colleagues to waive their demand, so that the work of the Conference might continue with the minimum of delay and disharmony. The second problem was connected with the engagement of interpreters. Insufficient attention had been paid to the security aspects of the use of interpreters, and a South African national had been included in the batch ordered through the Commission for Technical Cooperation in Africa south of the Sahara (CCTA). The United Nations however provided a suitable replacement following an urgent request.[38]

A working committee of officials from all the participating countries was set up, headed by A. L. Adu.

The following is a brief resumé of the proceedings of the Conference:

15 April

On the first day of the Conference Parliament House was full of diplomatic personnel. Only the French Ambassador was absent, being represented by his deputy (owing to the Algerian problem). As each delegation entered Parliament House it was met by Nkrumah. Nkrumah declared the Conference open, after he had been unanimously elected Chairman, and invited delegates to address the gathering.

Ethiopia:
Prince Sahle Selassie Haile-Selassie, son of the Emperor, announced that his 'illustrious father' wished to make the offer of fifty scholarships over a four-year period for students from all parts of Africa in Ethiopian institutions. He was followed by Ato Abebe Reta, Minister of Commerce, who expressed regret that 'the free people of Africa represented but one-third of the total population of the continent . . . We must remember that Africa alone . . . produces over 60 per cent of the world's gold, over 60 per cent of the world's uranium, and over 90 per cent of the world's radium'.

Libya:
Dr Wahbi Elbury said 'Peace in Africa could not be assured without regard to justice and equity for African problems'.

Liberia:
President W. S. Tubman said 'I think I voice the sentiments of us all when I say it is regrettable that the bulk of our 170 million people are still subject to foreign rule, and because their heritage is not their own, are unable to be represented in our deliberations.' They had come to the Conference, he said, 'not to partition any portion of the earth's surface but to advance the interest and welfare of the peoples of Africa'.

Morocco:
Sayed Mohamed Ahmed Balafrej, Minister of Foreign Affairs, told the Conference its just aim should be to come 'to the rescue of those of our friends who are fighting for their freedom'. He made specific reference to the Algerian

struggle which he described 'as an obstacle to the harmonious development of northern Africa'. One of the principal objectives of the King of Morocco and his government was the union of the countries of North Africa.

Egypt:

Dr Mahmoud Fawzy, Minister of Foreign Affairs, said 'The very convening of this Conference is a symbol of our times, and a most notable milestone on humanity's road ... to heal their air and wider horizons; the struggle for freedom should continue'.

Tunisia:

Dr Sadok Mokadden, Secretary of State for Foreign Affairs, spoke about the need for the colonial powers to have a necessary conversion in their relationships with the colonial peoples; he emphasized the determination of peace in North Africa and for the realization of the legitimate hopes of the Algerian people.

Sudan:

Sayed Mohamed Ahmed Mahgoub, Foreign Minister, spoke of the need for cooperation in all fields among independent African nations, and the encouragement of liberation movements in the independent territories of the African continent.

Ghana:

Nkrumah said that the purpose of the Conference was to enable the states represented to know one another and exchange views on matters of common interest; to endeavour to safeguard and consolidate their independence; to emphasize the need for study and developing the resources of Africa and for cooperative action among independent African states.

16 April

Private Session: Messages to the Conference were received from the United States Secretary of State (the first to be received at the Conference), the Prime Minister of the People's Republic of China, and Dr Nnamdi Azikiwe, Prime Minister of Eastern Nigeria. In the United States message Mr Dulles said he looked forward to the success of the Conference and pledged America's support for the constructive effort of the states of Africa to achieve a stable, prosperous community conscious of their interdependence within the family of nations and dedicated to the ideals of the United Nations Charter. After these messages, the issue before the Conference was the question of the reception to be accorded to the Algerian representation at the Conference. The UAR wanted them seated as observers but all the other delegations opposed this proposal. It was finally agreed that the Algerians should be allowed to present their case to the Conference while not being admitted as participants within the body of the Conference.

17 April

A message from Moscow containing congratulations from the President of the

USSR was received, as were cables from African nationalist organizations, and from the Palestinian Arabs.

General agreement was reached on solidarity with the Algerians but there was no consensus on the UAR proposal to supply arms direct to Algeria.

Dr Felix Roland Moumie, exiled leader of the French Cameroons, domiciled in Cairo, reported to the Conference.

18 April

The Algerian issue was settled. The Conference unanimously agreed to recognize the right of the Algerians to independence, deplored bloodshed in Algeria, urged France to withdraw its troops and to negotiate with the Algerian Liberation Front, and pledged full support to the Algerian cause. The issue of direct aid to Algeria was unresolved.

19 April

The Algerian issue now resolved and the UAR proposal finally rejected, the Conference agreed that a mission should be sent as soon as possible to world capitals to insist, in the name of Africa, that Algeria's independence should be recognized.

The questions of the French Cameroons and French Togoland were disposed of as follows:

(a) *Cameroons:* France's use of military force in the Cameroons was condemned: she was called upon to observe the principle of international trusteeship and to satisfy the legitimate aspirations of the peoples of the Cameroons by opening direct negotiations with their representatives.

(b) *Togoland:* The Conference recommended that France should cooperate fully with the United States commissioner in order to ensure fair and democratic elections.[39]

20 April

The Conference continued in committee; one of the decisions taken was that 15 April (opening day of the Conference) should be celebrated every year throughout the continent as Africa Freedom Day.[40]

21 April

The session continued with the delicate problem of aid to Algeria still unresolved.

22 April

The Conference ended with the passing of resolutions in which the Palestine issue was dealt with as part of a ten-point declaration under the subject of International Peace and Security; this specifically expressed deep concern over 'non-compliance' with United Nations resolutions, and called on member states of the United Nations to respect such resolutions; it further expressed deep concern over the question of Palestine which was seen as a disturbing factor in world peace and security.

Nkrumah's closing speech, among others, reflected the general feeling of success at the Conference: 'It is certainly not a figure of speech when I say that if formerly the Sahara divided us, this is certainly not the case today. The former imperialist powers were then all talking about "Arab Africa" and "Black Africa", about "Islamic Africa" and "non-Islamic Africa", about "Mediterranean Africa" and "Tropical Africa". These were artificial descriptions which tended to divide us. At this Accra Conference, these tendencies and discriminating epithets are no longer applicable. Today the Sahara is a bridge uniting us. We are one, of an entity symbolised by our united African personality'. At the end of the session it was agreed that the Conference should be convened biennially in different African capitals. The next one was to be held in Ethiopia in 1960. The African states also agreed to maintain permanent representatives at the United Nations. This machinery for consolidation has persisted to this day.

These details have been given at length to emphasize one important fact—the extent to which the administrative arrangements laid down for it contributed to its success.[41]

APPENDIX B

The arrangements for the 1965 OAU Conference in Accra touched the high water mark in the administration of international conferences in Ghana. The various committees set up to provide for the diverse needs of the Conference worked with clockwork precision. In 1958 only eight African states had met in Accra. In 1965, some seven years later, Ghana had developed such experience in the running of conferences that she was able to provide for some thirty-five states.

In less than ten months 'Job 600' was built and furnished for the Conference.

Details of the arrangements were as follows:

Entry Permits: special entry permits were issued for admission to State House and the Conference Hall. All heads of state were accommodated in spacious individual suites at State House. Permits were issued only by the Chief Administrator of the Conference Secretariat to delegates and others who sought admission to the Conference area.

Simultaneous Interpretation: The official languages of the Conference were English, French, and Arabic, and simultaneous translation was provided in all three languages. Delegates were requested to hand to the Conference Officer on duty four copies of all prepared speeches and the text was made available to the interpreters before the speech was delivered. After the delivery of each speech, a team of précis writers used the text to help speed up the issue of the record of meetings.

Car Parking: Provision was made in the grounds of State House for the parking of up to forty cars for heads of state. Accommodation was provided elsewhere for over seven hundred and fifty additional cars.

Conference Business: Admission to the main Conference floor and to the gallery was arranged for delegations on the following basis:

- 5 seats for each Delegation in the main auditorium.
- 2 seats for each Delegation in the gallery.
- 2 seats in the gallery for observer delegations and for Freedom Fighters.

Pressmen and invited guests were allowed room in the gallery during *public sessions.*

During *Committee sessions* three seats were provided for each delegation.

Press: Accredited pressmen and journalists were admitted to the Press Centre where they were able to work and attend press conferences. The press were accommodated at the University of Ghana, Legon (about eight miles from Accra), and were transported to the Conference and back daily by bus.

Accommodation for Delegates other than Heads of State: All Foreign Ministers, including their principal advisers, were accommodated at the Ambassador Hotel but their delegates and officials were housed in the Star Hotel and at the University of Ghana. These arrangements covered twenty-five delegates from each of the participating states.

Transport: Every head of state at the Conference was provided with a personal chauffeur-driven car with motor cycle escort and military ADC. The chauffeurs were carefully selected for their driving experience and knowledge of the city and its environs. For other members of each delegation three cars were provided with approved drivers and guides. In addition to these facilities the State Transport Corporation made provision for three saloon cars and two mini-buses as a standby for use at Summit House by household officials and staff. Where delegations required transport over and above the official allocations they were advised about the use of hired cars and taxis outside the public transport system. The reception halls of the two hotels and the Unisity gave clear directions as to the arrangements for such hire services.

Medical Facilities: A twenty-four hour medical service was set up at State House. Three general practitioners and six nurses were assigned for duty and worked in rotation. Senior medical officers at the Ridge Hospital and the Military Hospital were instructed to stand by for any cases likely to be referred to them. In addition one senior medical officer was assigned to each group of six heads of state/government.

The Conference failed to fulfil Nkrumah's expectations. The deliberations showed that the idea of setting up a continental union government was still remote from the political thinking of his colleagues in Africa. But politicians do not always see that their ambitions, whether for themselves or their people, are not often achieved overnight. Political development is a slow painful process. It takes directions not always favouring those who set them afoot. Once an idea has been sown, however, it dies hard—and it may eventually come to light in unexpected circumstances.

As far as the Secretariat was concerned the results of the Conference should be judged from another standpoint: the framework of administration had met one of its greatest challenges and had proved itself equal to its task.

APPENDIX C

An International Conference on the Law of the Sea is to be held in Geneva from 12 to 15 September ——.

(1) The Legal Division of this Office has consulted the Law Officers' Department on the present state of this Law, and advice has been given that Ghana's interests would be best served if the Law took account of the following considerations:

    (a)
    (b)
    (c)

(2) The present position on the Law of the Sea is provided in the attached memorandum a summary of which is as follows:

    (a)
    (b)
    (c)
    (d)

(3) It is necessary to stress the points in para. 1 above, with the object of securing support for an amendment to the present Law. Ghana's participation at the Conference is therefore essential. Our preliminary enquiries have elicited that of the twelve countries that are likely to attend the meeting, at least eight would support the Ghana line. These include Nigeria, Ethiopia, Cuba.

(4) It is proposed for your approval that the delegation should be composed as follows:

    (i) Mr K, Minister of Justice (leader of Delegation)
    (ii) Mr S, MP, Barrister-at-Law
    (iii) Mr Y, Retired Senior Civil Servant, formerly Head of the Ministry of Agriculture
    (iv) Mr O, Lecturer, Faculty of Law, University of Ghana

(5) The cost of attendance at this Conference is arrived at as follows:

(6) ? Approved.

(Signature of Officer)

(7) I have studied above Minute, I object to nomination of Mr Y because I consider that . . . I suggest that Mr E should take his place.

(Signature of Minister)

Minister
I approve

(Signature of PM/President)

APPENDIX D

Algeria:

A Ghana mission was formally established in Algiers in 1962, although while the Algerian struggle was still in progress Ghana had accorded Algeria *de facto* recognition in 1959 and *de jure* recognition in 1961; Ghana also made financial arrangements for an Algerian mission to be opened in Accra, before Algerian independence, with the late Frantz Fanon as Algeria's Ambassador.

Burundi:

An Embassy established in late 1964 after the visit of the Burundi Foreign Minister to Accra. The first Ambassador appointed by Nkrumah was a Bureau of African Affairs activist. For some time he used the communications facilities of the Ghana High Commission in Kampala.

Cameroon:

One of the last missions established by Ghana in December 1965 just before the coup. Although he had assisted Foncha with political advice and funds and encouraged him to seek unification with the French-speaking sector of the Cameroons, Nkrumah was never happy about the circumstances of Felix Moumie's mysterious death in Geneva. He distrusted Ahidjo as a protegé of the French authorities. Ahidjo on the other hand protested persistently against the presence of a large pro-Moumie faction in Ghana. The National Liberation Council closed the Ghana Embassy in 1966. It thus had a short-lived existence in the Cameroons.

Central African Republic:

No diplomatic relations.

Chad:

No diplomatic relations.

Congo Brazzaville:

Owing to Ghana's close association with Congo (Leopoldville) Kinshasa, Brazzaville was neglected. The Abbé Youlou, when President, was too pro-French to attract Nkrumah's attention or interest. Later, when Masemba-Debat became President, relations between the two countries improved.

Congo (Leopoldville) Kinshasa:
A politician, A. Y. K. Djin, was appointed in 1960. He had been Nkrumah's personal representative in the Congo long before the country attained independence. He thus became a very intimate associate of the Congolese political leaders, Lumumba, Kassavubu, Albert Kalonji, Gizenga, Mobutu, Kiwewa, and others.

Dahomey:
A mission was set up in 1962 at embassy level amid high expectations of close relations as a counter to the slow response of Togo to Ghana's attentions. President Maga was superficially cooperative (cf. his contribution at OAU), but expected financial assistance similar to loans given to Mali and Guinea. Ghana was at this time not so affluent herself. Maga was also subject to domestic and external pressure, particularly from Abidjan; Dahomey was more interested in a 'Benin Federation' involving Ghana, Togo, Dahomey, and Western Nigeria, but regionalism was political anathema to Nkrumah.

Ethiopia:
An embassy was established in 1959. The first Ghanaian Ambassador was M. A. Riberio who later served in the same capacity in Washington and Rome. He held the latter post until his retirement in 1969.

Gabon:
No diplomatic relations.

Gambia:
Before Gambia's independence Nkrumah maintained close personal relations with Garba-Jahumpa, whom he met in Manchester at the 1945 Pan-African Congress.

Guinea:
This post, owing to the Declaration of Union between Ghana and Guinea in November 1958, was opened as a Resident Ministry in January 1959. After the OAU Charter was inaugurated in May 1963, it became a normal embassy having an Ambassador.

Ivory Coast:
The establishment of diplomatic relations was agreed in September 1960. An Ambassador was appointed in March 1961. There was con-

siderable friction in Ghana-Ivory Coast relations owing to the presence of political exiles from both states in each other's capital. The differences between the two states were ideological. Houphouet-Boigny often said that his ancestors hailed from Ashanti in Ghana.

Kenya:

A Ghana High Commission was set up in Nairobi in December, 1963. It is noteworthy that up to the end of 1965, in spite of Ghana's close links with Kenya and Nkrumah's personal association with President Kenyatta, no Kenya mission had been set up in Ghana.

Liberia:

Diplomatic relations between Ghana and Liberia existed from Ghana's independence. For many years, and right up to the time of the coup in Ghana, Liberia's Ambassador was the Dean of the Diplomatic Corps.

Libya:

Ghana's mission in Tripoli from 1960 and for many years afterwards was occupied by a Chargé d'Affaires; Libya did not appoint a representative to Ghana.

Malagasy Republic:

No diplomatic relations.

Malawi:

Although Dr Banda had received financial aid from Nkrumah for his political campaigns in Nyasaland (*The Ghana Times* of 8 April 1959, records one grant of £10,000) he showed little inclination towards Ghana when his country secured independence.

Mali:

A resident Minister was appointed in December 1960, after the visit of Nkrumah to Bamako in November 1960. Mali was a member of the Ghana–Guinea–Mali Union.

Mauretania:

Relations existed between 1964 and 1965.

Morocco:

An embassy was established in the autumn of 1961. Between King Mohammed V and President Nkrumah there were very intimate personal relations. I once heard the President say that King Mohammed wished him to regard his son (Prince Hassan) as his younger brother and ward. The King gave Nkrumah a personal gift of a villa in Rabat, although Nkrumah never used it.

Niger:
   An embassy was opened in 1962 with a Chargé d'Affaires. The Niger government appointed an Ambassador to Ghana in 1961.

Nigeria:
   Ghana set up a commission in 1959 when Nigeria was still a dependent territory. This was elevated to High Commission status on the attainment of Nigeria's independence on 1 October 1960.

Rwanda:
   An embassy was established in 1965. Rwanda had no mission in Ghana.

Senegal:
   An embassy was set up in 1961, but the mission was maintained by a Chargé d'Affaires until 1962 when an Ambassador, Dr Foli, a Paris-educated political economist, was appointed.

Sierra Leone:
   As in Nigeria, a Ghana commission was opened here in 1960, prior to Sierra Leone's independence. This was raised to the status of High Commission in April 1961, to accord with Sierra Leone's independence.

Somalia:
   An embassy was established headed by a Chargé d'Affaires in 1961 followed by an Ambassador before the end of that year. Somalia did not have a diplomatic mission in Ghana.

Sudan:
   Diplomatic relations were established at embassy level in 1959.

Tanzania:
   A High Commission was set up by Ghana in Dar-es-Salaam in 1962. Tanzania had no diplomatic mission in Ghana between 1957 and 1965.

Togo:
   Diplomatic relations were established in 1963 at embassy level.

Tunisia:
   An embassy was set up in Tunis in 1960.

Uganda:
A High Commission was established in Kampala in 1963.

UAR:
A Ghanaian Ambassador presented his credentials to President Nasser in May 1958, a little over a year after Ghana's independence. Israel had set up a consulate in Accra even before the proclamation of independence in March 1957.

Upper Volta:
Diplomatic relations were established in 1961 at embassy level.

Zambia:
Ghana set up a mission in Lusaka in 1963.

APPENDIX E

GHANA'S DIPLOMATIC REPRESENTATION
OUTSIDE AFRICA TO 1965

Albania:
This mission, established in January 1962, would not have been necessary for political and diplomatic reasons. Having given the 'blanket' order for missions in Eastern Europe, Nkrumah would have been embarrassed by failure to establish one at Tirana.

Australia:
A Commonwealth state. Diplomatic relations were arranged soon after Ghana's independence.

Belgium:
Relations with Belgium, established in 1960, were erratic because of the Congo crisis. Initially cordial, although not without a degree of suspicion on both sides, they were broken at the end of that year and not re-established until 1962. Ghana did not assign an Ambassador to Belgium until 1965. Even then, he was resident in The Hague. Belgium was very badly served by her first representative, Mr Walravens, notorious in diplomatic circles and Accra society as a philanderer.

Brazil:
A mission in Brazil (opened in 1962) was of economic and cultural, rather than political, importance. The country is an effective rival to Ghana as a world cocoa producer. It also had a large African population, with distinct ethnic relations with the Ewe tribe (first-hand evidence of Bensah, former Ewe Minister who led a Ghana delegation to Brazil).

Bulgaria:
A mission was established in 1962 in the aftermath of Nkrumah's Eastern European tour.

Canada:
One of the Commonwealth posts established in 1957 shortly after independence. A High Commissioner was, however, not appointed until 1961.

Ceylon:
A Commonwealth state. The first Ghana High Commissioner was the Rev S. G. Nimako. Ceylon reciprocated by providing the first woman diplomat in Ghana, Mrs Senaratne.

China:
Established in 1960 with Ohenenana Cobina Kessie as Ghana's envoy. For Ghanaians, because of its austerity and remoteness from Africa, this post was regarded almost as penal. Those who accepted service there received considerable respect.

Cuba:
An embassy was established in 1960. There was a general feeling of mutual respect between Fidel Castro and Nkrumah in the context of Afro-Asian-Latin American solidarity against imperialism and colonialism. Che Guevara visited Ghana in 1965.

Czechoslovakia:
An embassy was established in 1962 in furtherance of Nkrumah's Eastern European policy. As, apart from Eastern Germany, this is the most prosperous state among the Soviet Eastern allies, it would have been deserving of Ghana's diplomatic attentions anyway.

Denmark:
Ghana had no mission in Denmark until 1966, although the Danish government had appointed its representative in Ghana as far back as 1961. At the time of the Ghana coup the Danish envoy was a woman, the first European female diplomat in Accra. The tardiness in establishment of a mission in Copenhagen was a reflection of Ghana's assessment of its economic and political importance.

France:
An embassy was set up in 1957 soon after independence. Until 1959 the Ghana High Commissioner in London represented Ghana's interest in Paris. Sir Edward O. Asafu-Adjaye fulfilled this dual role with marked competence.

German Democratic Republic:
In compliance with the 'Halstein Doctrine' Ghana maintained only a Trade Mission in East Germany. This was, of course, a diplomatic camouflage for the trade representatives of both states were to all intents and purposes, except in diplomatic status, national representatives.

German Federal Republic:
An embassy opened in 1959.

Hungary:
One of the Eastern European states which became diplomatically linked to Ghana in 1962 after Nkrumah's tour of Eastern Europe in 1961.

India:
A Commonwealth state. A High Commission was established after Ghana's independence and there had been a long period of pre-independence association.

Israel:
An embassy was set up in 1958 although Israel established a full mission at ambassador level in 1957. Before independence, Israel had a small consulate in the Gold Coast.

Italy:
An embassy was set up in 1961. No effort was made to establish formal links with the Vatican. This could have been achieved by accreditation of the Ghanaian envoy in Rome and would have involved additional expenditure but might have been a reasonable concession to the religious sentiment of the large Catholic population of Ghana. The present Pope, as Cardinal Montini, visited Ghana before his elevation to the Papacy.

Japan:
An embassy was established mainly for economic reasons in January 1960.

Lebanon:
Lebanon had an envoy in Ghana by 1960. From June 1959 it had maintained a legation. There has long been a large Lebanese and Syrian trading community in Ghana. Ghana did not establish a mission in Beirut. The National Liberation Council appointed an envoy to the Lebanon in 1966.

Mexico:
This mission was opened in 1964 for cultural reasons and within the framework of African-Latin American solidarity.

Netherlands:
An embassy office was set up in 1965. There has been a Royal

Netherlands envoy in Ghana since January 1959. The same reason as for Denmark obtains for the late opening of an embassy.

Pakistan:
A Commonwealth country. A Ghana High Commissioner was posted to Karachi in 1962.

Poland:
An embassy was established in 1962.

Romania:
An embassy was established in 1962.

Switzerland:
An embassy was set up in 1965. There was also a permanent UN Mission from 1959.

Turkey:
The National Liberation Council appointed an envoy in 1966; Ambassador resident in Rome.

USSR
Diplomatic relations were established in 1959; an embassy was set up in 1960.

United Kingdom:
A High Commission was set up on Independence Day 6 March 1957.

United Nations:
A Permanent Mission was established in September 1957. Major Seth Anthony was the first Ghanaian representative.

North Vietnam:
Diplomatic relations were established in 1965.

Yugoslavia:
An envoy was posted in 1960, but relations were established between the two states in 1959. There was a strong personal link between the two Presidents on the basis of their non-alignment policy.

Ghana had no missions in Indonesia, Iraq, the Philippines, Saudi Arabia, and Sweden, although these states had established diplomatic missions in Accra. The Swedish representative was resident in Monrovia. At no time did diplomatic relations exist with Singapore, Malaysia, or New Zealand, all Commonwealth countries.

BIBLIOGRAPHY

Adu, A. L., *The Civil Service in Commonwealth Africa* (London, 1969).
Apter, D. E., *The Gold Coast in Transition* (Princeton, 1955).
Bing, Geoffrey, *Reap the Whirlwind* (London, 1968).
Birmingham, W., et al., *Study of Contemporary Ghana: The Economy of Ghana* (London, 1966).
Blundell, Michael, *So Rough a Wind* (London, 1964).
Bretton, H. L., *The Rise and Fall of Kwame Nkrumah* (New York, 1966).
Dei-Anang, Michael, *Ghana Resurgent* (Accra, 1964).
—, 'Africa's Past and Present', *The Pan-Africanist Review*, vol. i, no. 1 (1964).
De Gregore, R., *Technology and the Economic Development of the Tropical African Frontier* (Cleveland, 1969).
Fleming, W. G., 'American Political Science and African Politics', *The Journal of Modern African Studies*, vol. vii, no. 3 (1969), pp. 495–510.
Ghana, *Report of the Conference of the Independent African States* (Accra, 1958).
Ghana, *A New Charter for the Civil Service* (Accra, 1960).
Gold Coast, *Final Report of the Working Party to Review the Africanization Programme* (Accra, 1953).
Gold Coast, *A Statement on the Programme of the Africanization of the Public Service* (Accra, 1954).
Gordon Walker, Patrick, *The Commonwealth* (London, 1962).
Hutchinson, Alfred, *Road to Ghana* (New York, 1961).
Legum, Colin, 'The Accra Conference', *Africa South*, vol. ii, no. 4 (1958), pp. 82–91.
Mackintosh, J. P., et al., *Nigerian Government and Politics* (London, 1966).
Nkrumah, K., *Ghana, The Autobiography of Kwame Nkrumah* (London, 1957).
—, *Africa Must Unite* (London, 1963).
—, *Neo-Colonialism* (London, 1965).
—, *Dark Days in Ghana* (London, 1968).
Odinga, Oginga, *Not Yet Uhuru* (London, 1967).
Padmore, George, *Pan-Africanism or Communism?* (London, 1956).
Tiger, L., 'Bureaucracy in Ghana: the Civil Service', unpublished PhD thesis, University of London, 1962.
Timothy, Bankole, *Kwame Nkrumah* (Evanston, Illinois, 1963).
Thompson, W. Scott, *Ghana's Foreign Policy, 1957–66* (Princeton, 1969).
Wallerstein, I., *Africa: The Politics of Independence* (New York, 1961).
Winstanley, M., 'Political Revolution in the Gold Coast: The Rise of the Petite Bourgeoisie', unpublished MA thesis, Institute of African Studies, University of Ghana, 1966.
Zartman, I. W., *The Politics of Trade Negotiations between Africa and the European Economic Community: The Weak Confront the Strong* (Princeton, 1971).

NOTES

1. The concept of a non-political civil service was seen by Nkrumah as colonialism's chief strategy for using 'indigenous administrators to run a regime that serves the interests of a foreign power'. *The Spark*, 5 April 1963, pp.1 and 6.

2. W. Scott Thompson, *Ghana's Foreign Policy: 1957–66*, pp. 424–5.

3. On this point, K. B. Asante, who saw my manuscript in draft, commented 'It would not be correct to state that the 1964 Conference in Cairo had "agreed to hold the 1965 meeting in Accra". In fairness to Dr Nkrumah, it should be indicated that he did not originate the idea of inviting the Conference to Accra. Notes that I made at that time indicate that it was some of his enthusiastic followers who advanced the idea and he reluctantly agreed. These enthusiasts ignored official advice that no invitation should be issued until Ghana was in possession of the appropriate facilities. In fact, it was Nkrumah who, confronted with the *fait accompli*, came down to earth and initiated consideration of the question of facilities.' This is perhaps a clear example of Nkrumah's readiness to take the initiative in moments of crisis which distinguished him from his colleagues. It seemed to me at the time that he had been gravely disturbed by the failure of the Conference to endorse his union government proposals for Africa. He was glad of the opportunity for yet another attempt at the Conference in Accra.

4. From a note by A. L. Adu dated 10 July 1972.

5. See Chapter 3.

6. *Transition* (Kampala), vol. vi (1966).

7. *Not Yet Uhuru*, p.185.

8. W. G. Fleming, 'American Political Science and African Politics', pp. 495–510.

9. Review, *The Journal of Modern African Studies*, vol. iv, no. 3 (1966), p.384.

10. Michael Blundell in *So Rough a Wind* indicated that the British in Kenya included some high-placed Africans among the 'haves' in administration to maintain their power. Such Africans opposed changes which facilitated development but threatened their own positions.

11. From the *Final Report of the Working Party to Review the Africanization Programme* to the committee consisting of A. L. Adu (Chairman), David Anderson, Michael Dei-Anang, Ivor G. Cummings (Secretary).

12. On the issue of Nkrumah's initial distrust of the army, police, and civil service at independence, see his *Dark Days in Ghana*, pp. 38–9.

13. George Padmore was a West Indian journalist who dedicated his life to the anti-colonial struggle during a long stay in Britain. Padmore and Nkrumah met at the Fifth Pan-African Congress in Manchester in 1945. It is perhaps singularly unfortunate that he is often remembered more for his early Communist sympathies than for his pan-Africanist ideology as a factor in decolonization. His *Pan-Africanism or Communism?* has a notable passage about his loss of faith in Communism: 'In our struggle for national freedom, human dignity and social redemption, Pan-Africanism affords an ideological alternative to Communism . . . No self-respecting African wishes to exchange his British masters for Russian ones.'

14. Thompson, op. cit., p. 29, where he states that Adu's opposition to Padmore's appointment was based on the fact that Adu believed that 'a West Indian could hardly have anything to teach them [i.e. Ghanaians] about Africa'.

15. From July 1960 under the new republican constitution such appointments were made by the President.

16. Reference to my making the travel plan for our delegation may appear somewhat trivial, in view of the importance attached to the Conference itself. This should be considered, however, in the light of the virtual isolation of the Gold Coast under colonial rule from the rest of the world.

17. Thompson, op. cit., p.29.

18. *Study of Contemporary Ghana: The Economy of Ghana*, p. 19.

19. Thompson, op. cit., p.250.

20. Immanuel Wallerstein, *Africa: The Politics of Independence*, p. 106. On the general question of Nkrumah's views concerning Africa's economic fragility, see his *Africa Must Unite* and *Neo-colonialism*; also R. De Gregore, *Technology and the Economic Development of the Tropical African Frontier*, and I. W. Zartman, *The Politics of Trade Negotiations between Africa and the European Economic Community: The Weak Confront the Strong*.

21. A. K. Barden was one of the most energetic characters during the closing years of Nkrumah's regime. He was an ex-serviceman and was first brought into prominence in Ghanaian affairs by his appointment as George Padmore's secretary in Accra. After Padmore's death he was promoted over the heads of several senior CPP functionaries to the Directorship of the Bureau of African Affairs. In this position, in addition to his other duties, he produced a series of articles on topical questions, including 'Evolution of Ghanaian Society', *Voice of Africa* (February 1964), pp. 24–7, and 'Nationalism and Newly Independent African States', *The Pan-Africanist Review*, vol. 1, no. 1 (1964), pp. 13–17.

22. Thompson, op. cit.

23. O & M Bulletin (no. 4, October 1962).

24. Cf. Thompson, op. cit., p. 448, and H. L. Bretton, *The Rise and Fall of Kwame Nkrumah*, pp. 184–5.

25. Nkrumah never called me 'Michael', my first name. This would have gone against the grain for a man who shed his own foreign name, 'Francis', to assume his African name 'Kwame'. It didn't worry him to call Bing 'Geoffrey' or simply 'Geoff' because, being British, he had no African alternative.

26. 'Neo-colonialism' was, of course, not coined by Nkrumah. What he really meant was that he had helped to give the term greater significance in African politics. He was certainly one of the first heads of state to do so.

27. It was generally supposed that persons who were responsible for arranging appointments with the President were instrumental in giving or withholding access to him. Officers who were known to be in positions of authority in Flagstaff House were therefore often blamed—usually without cause—for preventing access to, or allowing only their friends to see, the President. Individual officers, such as Erica Powell, the President's Private Secretary during a considerable part of his regime, E. K. Okoh, T. K. Impraim, Cabinet Secretary and Deputy Cabinet Secretary respectively, and sometimes myself were occasionally blamed in this manner. This is regrettable, for the President himself laid down detailed procedures governing the routine for appointments and no one had authority to contravene them without his consent. For example, as Head of the African Affairs Secretariat, I could not arrange for another departmental officer not a member of the Secretariat to call on the President. This point may be further illustrated by a personal example. An uncle of mine, Opanyin Odei Mensah, was the chief cocoa farmer in the Eastern section of Akwapim District. Knowing my position as Senior Secretary in Flagstaff House he constantly urged me to arrange for him to see the President on cocoa matters. I found it difficult to get him to understand

that I could not do this for him without exposing myself to charges of partiality towards him because of our relationship, and that, for him, the normal channel of communication was through Martin Appiah Dankwa, then General Secretary of the Ghana Farmers' Council. It was only after the military coup took place that he confided to me that he was now in a position to appreciate the lesson I had tried all the time to teach him about the chain of responsibility.

28. See Nigeria *Debates*, 28 March 1962, cols 408–14; also J. P. Mackintosh, *Nigerian Government and Politics*, where the author reports that in discussing apartheid in South Africa and the Portuguese colonies Nigeria had begun to speak in terms 'not far removed from those of President Nkrumah'. See also Odinga, op. cit., p. 186: 'It was in Cairo that we made our first contact with liberation figures in other parts of the Continent, among them, Felix Moumie of the Cameroons, Kenneth Kaunda, Chipembere, Simon Kapepwe, Joshua Nkomo and the Rev Sithole. Dr Mohamed Fayek, the UAR Director-General of African Affairs gave us invaluable assistance in assembling a press and making Pan-African contacts.'

29. Ibid., p.189. 'I appealed to President Nasser to help in the launching of our national press, and he promised financial support for our struggle.' Alfred Hutchinson, a South African Coloured, one of the accused in South Africa's mass treason trials, who had fallen in love with a white woman, set as his goal with his love a daring escape to the 'New Nation of Ghana, 3000 or more miles North, for nowhere short of there could they feel secure . . . The first lights of ACCRA wink below, and the engines ease off, relax. I am filled with gratefulness. Grateful that there is in the world a place like Ghana. Grateful for the sheltering arm.' (Alfred Hutchinson, *Road to Ghana*.) Ronald Segal, who is now a publisher and journalist in Britain, is one of a number of white South African liberals who, with the assistance of the Ghanaian government, made their way to freedom through this Ghana gateway.

30. See Odinga, op. cit., p.222. 'I had my passport returned, though it had to be surrendered immediately. I got back to Kenya. I should here mention my warmest appreciation to Kwame Nkrumah and his Ghana Government who, when my passport was recalled, issued me with a Ghana laissez-passer that made me the most respected of travellers at a time when my own country was penalizing me.'

31. The late Sir Samuel Quashie-Idun, who became President of the Court, and Mr Justice Azu-Crabbe. Sir Samuel was then serving as Chief Justice of Western Nigeria and was therefore nominated by the government of Nigeria. Mr Azu-Crabbe was a nominee of Nkrumah.

32. For a detailed discussion of the 'African personality' see chapter 11 of my *Ghana Resurgent*.

33. See David Apter, *The Gold Coast in Transition*; also Geoffrey Bing, *Reap the Whirlwind*; M. Winstanley, 'Political Revolution in the Gold Coast: the Rise of the Petite Bourgeoisie'.

34. Patrick Gordon Walker, in *The Commonwealth*, p. 69, wrote about the whole question as follows: 'The great achievement of the nation-builders of Ghana and Nigeria was not so much that they created national feeling within frontiers that ran through tribes and families; but that, within the boundaries, they fused together so many diverse tribal and religious entities, and inspired them with a sense of nationhood that was sufficient to secure independence from British rule. This independence was achieved only because the leaders of the independence movements succeeded, as in other Commonwealth countries, in casting the demand for national freedom in a parliamentary democratic form. Thereby, they not only

gave a cohesive structure to the emerging nations, but at the same time thrust the independence movement on a course that inevitably led to national freedom.' This sounds very British indeed but settles very little in Ghana or in Nigeria, as the breakdown of the constitutional structures based on parliamentary models in both countries (and other parts of Africa) seems to suggest.

35. Bing, op. cit., p.191.

36. On the role of the African civil servant, A. L. Adu, who, as has already been noted, was one of the most outstanding African civil servants, has commented as follows: 'I could not agree more with the views stated in this chapter which accord with my own experience of working not only under Nkrumah, but also with Presidents Nyerere, Obote, and Kenyatta. In fairness to the Ghana civil service, however, one should state that its leaders were constantly aware of the need to achieve a meeting of minds, an effective "tuning-in" to the political language and policy pronouncements of the Government . . .'

37. 'Bureaucracy in Ghana: the Civil Service.'

38. See *Report of the Conference of the Independent African States*, pp. 763 and 767.

39. As indicated in an earlier chapter, these elections were held and resulted in the independence of the territory from France.

40. This date was observed as agreed until the OAU was established in May 1963, when the new day (25 May) of the OAU Conference superseded it.

41. For further information on the Accra Conference, see Colin Legum, 'The Accra Conference'. In a debate in the National Assembly, Mr Victor Owusu (UP, Agona Kwabre) called in question the government attitude to unemployment at home, bad trade, and street begging. He cited as examples of government extravagance expenditure on travel by the Prime Minister, the purchase of a Rolls-Royce, and the spending of £73,000 on the Conference of Independent African States (Ghana, *National Assembly Debates*, 2 July 1958).

INDEX

Accra Conference 1958, 45, 64–8
Accra Conference 1965, *see* Organization of African Unity
Adamafio, Tawia, 59, 60, 61
Adjei, Ako, 1, 17, 25n, 28, 51, 59, 60
Adu, A. L., ix, 10, 11, 12–13, 17, 25n, 34n, 40
African administration, viii–ix, 8, 55–63
African Affairs Secretariat, 1, 4, 5, 8, 18–19, 24–38, 40, 42–3, 47–8
Amonoo, H. R., 3, 26, 36
Arkhurst, Fred, 11, 12, 17, 54
Armah, Kwesi, 43, 53
Asante, K. B., ix, 3, 5, 18, 25n, 26, 31n, 36, 44, 59n, 61

Bandung Conference, 19–20
Barden, A. K., 25n, 26, 29, 30–1, 41–42
Bing, Geoffrey, 24, 49, 51, 56
Boateng, Kweku, 24, 50, 51
Botsio, Kojo, 7, 17, 19, 20, 31n, 43, 44, 50
British administrative model, vii–viii, 7; *see also* Colonial Administration
Bureau of African Affairs, 1, 4, 13, 18, 24, 25n, 26–31, 41–2

Casablanca Conference 1961, 25n, 45
Colonial Administration, vii, 7, 55–7
Commonwealth, 21, 51, 52, 53; foreign services of, vii, 1; Commonwealth Relations Office, 11; *see also* India
Congo Coordination Committee, 24, 25n
Consulates, 18, 22

Convention People's Party (CPP), ix, 7, 8, 40, 42, 55, 61
Coup of 1966, viii, 5, 62

Dei-Anang, Michael, 20; as Permanent Secretary of Ministry of Foreign Affairs (1959–61), 1, 7, 14, 17; as Head of African Affairs Secretariat (1961–6), 3, 8, 25n, 31, 35–8

Edusei, Krobo, 7, 51

Flagstaff House Secretariats, 2, 25, 30–32
Fleming, W. G., 7, 57
Foreign Service, structure, 16–17, 40–43; training in U.K., 1, 11; *see also* Missions abroad, Ministry of Foreign Affairs
Francophone Africa, 9, 15, 20, 26, 37, 44n, 52, 58–60
Freedom Fighters, *see* Liberation Struggle

Gardiner, Robert, 5
Gbedemah, 7, 50

Hodgkin, Thomas, ix, 8
Hooker, R., 21n

India, 14–15, 17, 20, 51

Kofi, A. B. B., 11, 17

Liberation Struggle, 4–5, 7, 13, 18, 24, 27, 29, 39